STARS BENEATH THE SEA

To Hans and Lotte Hass
who, although they didn't know it, first enticed me beneath the
waves.
And to Win,
whom I failed to drag down with me.

STARS BENEATH THE SEA

THE PIONEERS OF DIVING

TREVOR NORTON

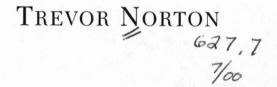

627.7
7/00

CARROLL & GRAF PUBLISHERS, INC.
NEW YORK

First Carroll & Graf edition 2000

Carroll & Graf Publishers, Inc.
A Division of Avalon Publishing Group
19 West 21st Street
New York, NY 10010-6805

Library of Congress Cataloging-in-Publication Data is available.

ISBN: 0-7867-0750-X

Manufactured in the United States of America

Contents

Acknowledgements

I am indebted to those who have generously guided me to the literature or shared their memories of the pioneers whose stories I have told. Especial thanks to Dr Nguyen Tac An, Nick Baker, Professor George Bass, Joseph Baur Jr, Dr John Bevan and Ann Bevan, Kevin Casey, Clive Cussler, Daniel David, Lynn Delgaty, Peter Dick, Professor David Elliot, Professor Jacques Forest, Honor Frost, Herb Greer, Dr Audrey Geffen, Dr Karl Gunnarsson, Dr Bob Hanson, Dr Val Hempleman, Nola Juraitis, Ginny Kuga, Pierre-Yves Le Bigot, Dr Colin Martin, Maura Mitchell, Marie-Thérèse Panouse, Sir John Rawlins, Philippe and Bernard Tailliez, John Towse, Roscoe Thompson, Nikos Tsouchlos, Reg Vallintine, Garren Wells, Reg Withey, and the library staffs of the American Museum of Natural History, *Daily Telegraph*, *The Independent*, *Los Angeles Times*, *San Francisco Chronicle*, and Liverpool University.

The responsibility for the translations from foreign language texts quoted in the book is mine, although on occasion I was helped by David Longet, and Gero Vella. Sincere thanks also to Jim Ludgate and Chris Bridge who made presentable pictures from inadequate originals, and Win Norton whose drawings adorn the chapter heads.

Before you submerge . . .

The art of diving is far from new. Long before history began, naked divers plunged into the Pacific and the Mediterranean. The science of diving came a little later.

Glaucus, who built the *Argo* in which Jason voyaged in search of the golden fleece, was a sponge diver. He ate a magic seaweed that allowed him to stay down longer. Perhaps he consumed too much, for one day he failed to return, as divers sometimes do.

Early divers searched the sea for sponges and clams or coral and mother-of-pearl, but there were two greater imperatives, the need to surprise an enemy and to salvage lost treasure.

Alexander the Great wished to inspect *all* the territory he had conquered and there is a painting of him encased in a glass barrel beneath the sea accompanied by a nervous cockerel and a cat. He capped all fishermen's tales in advance by observing a giant fish that took four days and nights to pass before his gaze.

Alexander's divers built underwater booms to defend a harbour; the Athenians used divers to breach the harbour booms at Syracuse during the Peloponnesian war in 415 BC. Herodotus describes how two Greek divers, Scyllias and his daughter, Cyana, cut the Persian fleet adrift and escaped by swimming nine miles under water, probably by breathing through short reeds. They were rewarded by having golden statues of themselves erected in the Temple of Delphi.

The ancient Romans had crack regiments of frogmen called *urinatores*. Knowing the habits of divers, perhaps the reason for this name should remain obscure. They certainly had odd habits, including going below with a mouthful of oil which they then spat out under water in order to 'catch a moment of breath', whatever that might mean.

There are many drawings from this period of divers wearing leather helmets with a long tube snaking up to a float on the surface far above. None of these could have worked for the diver cannot suck down air against the pressure differential even when only a couple of yards down. But Aristotle had presumably seen a practical snorkel when he wrote: 'Just as divers are sometimes provided with instruments through which they can draw air from above the water, and thus remain for a long time under the sea, so also have elephants been furnished by nature with their lengthened nostril, and whenever they have to pass through water they lift the nostril above the surface.'

For salvage work the diver would have to penetrate deeper and stay far longer than a lungful of air would allow.

Again it is Aristotle who records that sponge divers had inverted jars full of air lowered to them: 'These vases are forced steadily down, held perfectly upright, for if tipped slightly, the water enters.' Clearly, even in the fourth century BC the principle of the diving bell was understood. It was not, however, until 1599 that a large inverted cask with a man inside was successfully used under water. No less a figure than Edmund Halley, when not gazing at comets, designed a wooden bell large enough to carry several men to the sea floor. His innovation was to extend the

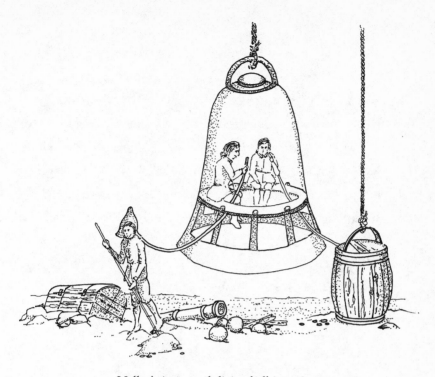

Halley's improved diving bell in action

divers' endurance by sending down barrels of air to replenish the supply. He also furnished a watertight hood and hose so that they could work outside the bell. Halley's bell became routinely used for underwater salvage work as much as 60 feet down and for 90 minutes at a time. In 1788 John Smeaton, having built the Eddystone lighthouse, designed the first practical pump that could supply a bell working at depth. Smeaton's steel box became the top-of-the-range diving bell for the next 150 years.

The traditional 'hard hat' metal helmet connected to a watertight suit of sheet rubber sandwiched between two layers of twill was invented by an Englishman, John Deane, in 1820, and its exploitation made Siebe Gorman of London the most famous manufacturer of diving equipment in the world. It was the first outfit that sealed off the diver from the elements and controlled the flow of air to him. The limit to its range was the depth to which sufficient air could be pumped, for it was the pressure of the air breathed by the diver that prevented him being crushed by the press of the water outside. The gear was so successful that in 1839 the Royal Navy founded the first ever diving school.

In *Twenty Thousand Leagues Under the Sea*, published in 1869, Jules Verne has the crew of the submarine, *Nautilus*, strolling unencumbered on the sea floor, collecting specimens, mining for minerals and even burying a dead comrade. Readers wondered at his imagination, but, as Captain Nemo explained, it was all possible. They used 'the Rouquayrol apparatus . . . which I have brought to perfection for my own use'.

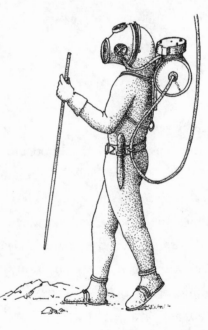

The Rouquayrol and Denayrouze diving gear

Four years earlier Benoît Rouquayrol, a mining engineer, and Auguste Denayrouze, a naval officer, designed a suit in which air was pumped down from the surface. But there was also a cylinder carried on the back containing pressurised air. The diver could detach himself from the air hose and wander free on the sea floor for short periods. The most important innovation, however, was a simple valve that not only supplied air at the pressure of the surrounding water, but did so only when the diver sucked on the mouthpiece, so it didn't waste the air supply. It was the means to untether the diver, but few appreciated it at the time. It was not until 1942 that Jacques Cousteau's collaborator, Émile Gagnan, reinvented this 'demand' valve and modern free-diving was born. At last there was a self-contained underwater apparatus (SCUBA) with which anyone could explore the underwater world.

Almost a hundred and forty years ago a French naval officer set out the regulations for his divers. They:

> should not be in a sweat
> should be in good health
> should be of a cool, calm temperament and
> must not be under the influence of alcohol.

If these rules were rigidly applied, it is surprising he ever mustered a team, for divers were rarely all, or indeed any, of these things.

In these safety-conscious days the rule book is heavier than the weight belt, but the pioneers of diving rarely conformed to rules. They were mavericks, energetic and eccentric visionaries who risked their lives for the thrill of discovery. Some began as spear fishermen, others as biologists or journalists or looters of reefs and wrecks. But under water they underwent a sea change.

This is the story of some of these extraordinary people.

THE WAY OF THE NATIVE

Native divers that searched for resources scattered over the sea floor needed to be mobile to cover as much ground as possible. They swam rather than walked, and descended head first. They were the first skin divers.

There was another route in the history of diving, one in which devices abounded and technology triumphed as man invented more complicated ways in which to drown. As we walked upright on land, so should the diver promenade under water, weighed down with lead collars and boots and the feeling that he might never see the surface again. Thus encumbered, the tethered and terrified diver descended into the depths.

Not surprisingly, it was the way of the native that would prove to be universally seductive, and one man above all others 'invented' skin diving for pleasure. His name was Guy Gilpatric.

Gilpatric all agog in goggles, Cap D'Antibes, late 1930s

A serious sinker

John Guy Gilpatric 1896–1950

Whilst living in the south of France in 1929, a New Yorker was the first man to become addicted to skin diving. He had intended to become a flyer and became briefly famous as a pilot prodigy, setting an altitude record of 4,665 feet over the Californian desert when he was only sixteen years old. In the following five years he became a qualified instructor, an exhibition flyer at air shows and then a test pilot.

At twenty-one he volunteered for the Air Service. Lieutenant Guy Gilpatric then joined the American Expeditionary Forces and was off to France for the last eighteen months of what was called 'the Great War', as if all previous conflicts left something to be desired.

He returned a captain and, unlike many of his buddies, without a scratch. On being demobilised he decided that his flying days were over and he would become a famous writer instead. After all, Henry James and Jack London had recently died and there was a vacancy. His first step on the ladder was as a copywriter at an advertising agency, but he hated being cooped up all day in a tiny office scribbling stuff in which he had not the slightest interest. Although he had no pretensions about his literary skills and later confessed that 'deficiencies were never known to deter me', he was convinced that he was a competent writer. So, peering through the splits in his infinitives, he became a freelance journalist. His articles were soon in demand and by 1920 he had earned enough to marry and decamp to a villa at Antibes on the French Riviera.

Gilpatric had shown little affinity for the sea, but now he lived beside the Mediterranean where the water was so transparent that from the cliff tops it was impossible to tell how much of the bone-white rocks were under water. The sea beckoned.

Antibes was where the beautiful people, and those who thought themselves to be beautiful, came to play and pose. Film scouts prowled the coast looking for pretty girls and they didn't have far to look. Directors assembled twitterings of starlets and shot featherweight movies by the sea. Everybody was having a grand time, except for Isadora Duncan, whose scarf connived with a car wheel to garrotte her.

Gilpatric, one of the less beautiful people, hit upon the idea of writing stories about the misadventures of the SS *Inchcliffe Castle*, a fictional rust bucket of an English merchant ship. Although he knew little about the merchant navy, the stories were published in the *Saturday Evening Post* and its readers loved the tales of Mr Glencannon, the Scottish ship's engineer, and the rest of the dissolute crew.

The public clamoured for more stories, but the *Post* couldn't get them. Gilpatric's editor complained that 'every Glencannon story had to be extracted under anaesthesia.'

Then a typescript arrived that held the clue to how Gilpatric had been spending his time. It was an article on diving. In 1929 Guy discovered spear fishing and disappeared under water. Against the editor's better judgement, the *Post* decided to publish the article in the hope that it would allow their star author 'to get octopuses out of his system and get back to Mr Glencannon'. It wasn't going to be quite as easy as that. Several other pieces on diving arrived – and the occasional Glencannon story to keep them quiet.

Back in France, Guy was diving every day, although his goggles leaked and the misaligned lenses gave him double vision. Lacking flippers and a weight belt, his diving technique was singular, but effective. 'He filled his lungs and swept a cupped hand into the water, then he bounced out to the waist, blew the air from his lungs, and sank rapidly, feet first. Under water, he turned and drove with quick kicks straight for the bottom, with his lungs squeezed towards crushing point . . .' In the early days he also wore a nose clip and stupidly plugged his ears against the pressure, which could have ruptured his eardrums; equalising the pressure, not defying it, is the secret.

His small group of 'serious sinkers' were mostly expatriates, armed with harpoons ten feet long, propelled by a thick rubber band like a slingshot. They trained hard to be at peak fitness. Gilpatric had a particularly rigorous regime: 'I had always lived the outdoor life when I wasn't in the house, never drinking any-thing stronger than whisky except vodka and rarely smoking more than one cigarette at a time.'

Hans Hass captured Gilpatric's hunting philosophy when he wrote: 'You confront the fish in its own element, where every advantage is on its side. It can swim faster, stay under water indefinitely, never suffers from earache, and needs no nose clip. The goggle-fisher's harpoon and his intellect are his only strong points, but . . . in battle with the great predatory fish of the sea the goggle-fisher has no advantage at all. Surely this is the height of fairness.'

After publication of the articles on diving in the *Saturday Evening Post*, Guy was inundated with letters from people who would like to learn to dive, and those who, until then, had thought they were the only ones that did. They caught the imagination of a group in San Diego who, in 1933, founded what was probably the first ever diving club, calling themselves The Bottom-Scratchers.

A teenage Hans Hass stumbled across Gilpatric hunting at Eden Roc, near to Cap d'Antibes:

> It was a marvellous day. Not a breath of air quivered over the hot cliffs, the sea was tired and gentle. Every now and then a wave would grumble, having gone astray in a cave . . .
>
> I noticed a human body among the rocks. It floated motionless on the surface, the head hanging under the water; at first I thought the man was dead. But then the head rose; the swimmer took breath. He wore rubber goggles over his eyes and in his right hand he had a long stick.
>
> I now watched the man disappearing from time to time beneath the waves. He . . . sank away absolutely without a sound, so that no waves betrayed where he had vanished. Each time it would be astonishingly long before he reappeared, somewhere, at quite another spot, as noiselessly and unexpectedly as he had gone, and never a sign of being out of breath.
>
> He had dived again . . . a big brown

creature below the waves . . . He swam remarkably carefully and cautiously, and pointed his stick at a coloured bunch of seaweed . . . A brief gleam in the water, then the man came to the surface. On his spear gleamed a fish, pierced through the middle!

The man finally came ashore . . . His skin was tanned by water and sun, his hair like a bundle of straw.

'A harpoon?' was his ready answer to my question. 'The best man to make you one is Martin the mechanic at Antibes. He wants three hundred francs. But don't go swimming alone in deep water, because sharks sometimes come over to the Cape here. And watch out for octopuses too!'

Then he thrust the knife with which he had killed the fish back into its sheath, pulled the goggles over his eyes, and vanished again into the sea.

In 1938 Gilpatric expanded the diving articles from the *Saturday Evening Post*, added tips from his readers and produced the first ever book on sports diving. 'If a few years ago anybody had predicted that one day I would write a book about catching fish for sport, I'd have scoffed . . . although I had . . . dangled a hook in many waters, I realised that the result was due neither to intelligence nor skill on my part, but only to the appetite of creatures I couldn't even see . . . Was fishing a sport? I had my doubts . . . And then I took up Goggling!'

The title page of his book says it all:

The Compleat Goggler
Being the First and Only Exhaustive Treatise
on the Art of
GOGGLE FISHING
That most Noble and Excellent Sport Perfected and
Popularized By
GUY GILPATRIC
in the Mediterranean Sea
Setting Forth the Proper manner of making the
GOGGLES, SPEARS and other Needful GADGETS
Together with
Descriptions of Many Marvels Witnessed
Upon the
BOTTOM OF THE SEA
And Fully Exposing the Author's Cunning Methods
of
Spearing Fish
&
Octopi

The title was, of course, a nod to Izaak Walton's classic text on fishing, published in 1653: *The Compleat Angler, or the Contemplative Man's Recreation. Being a Discourse of Fish and Fishing, not unworthy of the perusal of most anglers.*

Although both books instruct in the art of fishing and use it as a vehicle to describe the landscape and local natural history, they could not be more different. Walton rambles not only along the river bank, but into the world of gentle philosophy. He contemplates sticklebacks and scripture, perch and poetry, minnows and mythology and milkmaids' songs. Although his facts are sometimes erroneous, his imaginary companion was right to claim, 'Your discourse seems to be music and charms me to an attention.'

In contrast, *The Compleat Goggler* is a slick, slangy rollercoaster ride, 'an epic written as a vaudeville sketch'. One chapter is entitled: 'Garglings of a garrulous goggler, witnessing wonders, telling lies, exploring wrecks and hunting treasure'. There is even a chapter of recipes. *Octopus à la Niçoise* begins unpromisingly: 'When the octopus is dead, which he rarely is, he doesn't look much better than he looks when he's alive.' The provenance of some dishes is uncertain: '*Fish à la Monte*. I don't know the real name of this style of cooking fish, but my dog likes it this way as much as I do, so I have named it after him.'

The book is best taken in small doses, yet it undoubtedly captures those swashbuckling days when even those who were to become serious divers were diverted by the bloodthirsty pleasures of underwater hunting. And the book inspired them. Philippe Tailliez gave a copy to Cousteau and for decades it sailed in the Commandant's cabin on the *Calypso*.

Let us follow Gilpatric as he dips his aviator's eye into the sea for the first time:

> Then, suddenly, there came strange rumours. Somebody, somewhere, had evolved a radical and super-sportsmanlike manner of fishing – or, at least, so he claimed. His name . . . olde Guyzaak Gilpatric. His method, they said, was called goggle fishing . . .
>
> First, because so many fish go through life handicapped by names like scrod, chub, guppy

and squid, I must explain that goggle fishing
doesn't mean fishing for goggles . . . Goggle
fishing is fishing with a spear and watertight
eye-glasses – going down like McGinty to the
bottom of the sea . . . I made my first pair
myself from an old pair of flying goggles,
plugging up the ventilating holes with putty
and painting over them.

In goggle fishing the spear is thrust like a
sword and is never thrown, for you cannot
throw a spear much farther under water than
you can throw a motorbus on land . . .

I was unprepared for the breathtaking
sensation of free flight which swimming with
goggles gave me. It wasn't at all like flying in a
plane, where you are conscious of being borne
by something tangible . . . The bottom was
fifteen feet below me now, but every pebble
and blade of grass was distinct as though there
were only air between. The light was a soft
bluish-green – even restful, and somehow
wholly appropriate to the aching silence which
lay upon those gently waving meadows . . .

[On] the underside of a shelf, anchovies
and sardines – thousands of them – were
swimming around eating the foliage. But – I
rubbed my goggles – they were swimming on
their backs! . . . I dove right under the ledge,
where it was dark and cold, and shoo-ed the
whole crowd out. As soon as they left the
shadow and saw the sunlight above them, they

turned right side up and went their ways like
any self-respecting fish . . . those fish were not
aware that they were on their backs. They
thought that the ceiling was the floor, being in
practically the same fix as the old-time aviators
who, lacking instruments for flying in clouds
and fog, used to lose all sense of direction and
turn upside down without realising it until
loose objects, such as bottles, commenced
falling upwards out of the cockpit.

I had the sensation of flying in the chasm
of a New York street. Below me I saw vague
forms moving – fish . . . I hovered in suspense
which they didn't seem to share . . . Suddenly,
I found myself staring into the eyes of what
looked like a German U-boat – a three-foot
loup [bass] in a fine state of indignation, his
dorsal fin jutting up like the bristles of a
bulldog. Without stopping to think, I cut loose
my right and pasted him square on the jaw.

I came to the surface, gulped some air,
and pondered on the sorry state to which I
had fallen in being unable to knock out a
three-foot fish . . . I filled my lungs, swam
down a way and indulged in some
experimental shadow-boxing. I soon found the
trouble. Being lighter than water, my punches
simply pushed me backward, and the harder I
walloped, the faster I shoved myself away
from what I was aiming to hit. Also, I was
using a lot of energy in resisting my tendency

to float to the surface. I blew out my air, sank down farther, and uncorked a couple of rights and lefts. Now, I felt that my blows really had a little steam behind them. My body being heavier than water, my punches had something to react against . . .

As I swam towards the beach I thought of what I'd learned – namely, that some fish are not afraid of swimmers, and that to exert power under water you have to empty your lungs. It occurred to me that in these discoveries might lie the basis of a new sport. Still, I didn't feel that socking fish in the jaw was quite the way to do things, so I determined to buy a spear . . .

My first spear was a trident with piano-wire teeth forged into barbs. The handle was the handle of a hay-rake . . .

I spotted a school of slim, streamlined mullets . . . their sides flashing silver through the cloud of sand which their fins fanned up. Before I could get down to them, they spotted me and darted away . . . fish are more wary in the shallows than in the depths. Diving is their instinctive means of escape, and when this avenue is closed to them, they won't take chances.

I headed for a submerged rock and deep water . . . on the far side were *dorades* [giltheads]. Blowing out my air I sank down a way and then swam towards them: one lazed

away from the group . . . I lunged – and
missed him by a yard!

Well, the lunge had been short because I
hadn't bided my time and come close enough
to the fish . . . The *dorades* were still there. One
of them – he looked as big as a guitar – was
tearing mussels from the side of the rock and
chawing them horsily. I sank towards him.
The nearer I approached the more greedily he
ate, as though fearing that I intended to horn
in on his meal. Ten feet – eight feet – six.
There were the whites of his eyes. Now –
zippo – I let him have it!

The spear was yanked out of my grasp. I
grabbed it with both hands and tried to kick
my way up to the surface. I had to have air . . .
and as I shot upwards I saw the *dorade*
heading in the other direction. The heavy teeth
of my trident were bent and twisted like
hairpins . . .

Next day I put to sea with a spear which
would have held a walrus . . . I saw a grey fish
with dark tiger-stripes . . . I sank to meet him.
Our paths crossed just as he came within
range. I lunged and caught him fair and
square . . .

Well, my return to the beach with that
mourme [marmora bream] saw my stock rise
considerably in Juan-les-Pins . . . Next day,
when I brought in a two-foot *sargue* [white
bream] and a *dorade* weighing seven pounds, a

Gilpatric with his catch, late 1930s

considerable portion of the summer population
sprouted spears and goggles . . .

All summer long we'd had priceless sport
. . . we goggled for six hours a day . . . We had
learned things about fish and their habits
which certainly no fisherman and perhaps no
scientist had ever known . . .

We began to realise that certain
individual fish spend their time in fixed
neighbourhoods and that others, like some
migratory birds, come back to the same spot at
the same time year after year . . .

'I have often heard fish conversing in grunts like pigs,'
Gilpatric boasted, 'and listened to clicking as of fifty telegraph keys
in flat, calm water when there were no pebbles or any visible cause.
I have met fish supposed not to exist within miles of where I saw
them, and seen others which I was politely, but authoritatively told
did not exist at all.' Maybe so, but neither he nor his colleagues
were immune from divers' tales. One of the group, Alec
Kramarenko, speared a mullet. He brought it ashore, removed the
spear and dropped his catch on the sand. The stunned fish came
to, flopped into the water and swam rapidly out to sea. But clearly
his compass had been knocked awry for he turned around and shot
back, 'hit the sand at full speed and slid right up onto dry land at
Mr Kramarenko's feet'. Then there were the Blanchet brothers
who wrestled a big grouper for two hours before landing him.
When they got him home, he too sprang back into life, 'wrecked
the kitchen, chased Mother Blanchet three times around the parlour and ate a framed chromo-lithograph of the battle of
Austerlitz . . . before they could calm him with an axe'. Divers' tales

indeed or, as Shakespeare put it, 'Full fathom five thy father *lies*'.

Gilpatric and his companions rediscovered the snorkel and invented the dive mask. Kramarenko made a cast of his face so that he could mould his device to its contours. He constructed a face mask out of celluloid, dissolving photographic film in acetone and painting it layer by layer on to the cast. Then he made a lead mould into which he poured molten rubber. In 1937 he marketed the device, but his neighbour, Maxime Forjot, patented a mask that covered the nose as well as the eyes and thus obviated the problem of pressure squashing the mask against the face. The diver only had to snort into the mask to relieve the discomfort.

Kramarenko also produced a spring-loaded harpoon gun that could propel a four-foot spear several yards under water. Guy disapproved, for now 'any novice can hover on the surface and make a kill without even getting his hair wet.' The Serious Sinkers shifted location every day and rested a fished site for at least a week before returning. But now they had been joined by many 'Johnny-dive-latelys' armed with pitchforks and ski poles and Kramarenko's gun. An English yachtsman bought two guns and went hunting followed by a loader in a dinghy. He even employed beaters to drive the mullet towards him as if they were grouse. He caught seven hundred fish in a day. 'We were vastly cheered,' Gilpatric admitted, 'to learn that one of the gunmen had shot himself in the foot.'

Their favourite reef had been dynamited so the fish became timid and scarce, and on the crowded beaches, according to Cyril Connolly, 'fetid waves of sunburn oil lapped tidelessly on the sand.' Antibes became crowded with 'tarts, gigolos and motor car salesmen'. The idyll was coming to an end.

In 1939 the chill mistral wind came early. It ruffled the sea, rattled the awnings over the cafés and lifted the skirts of the palms. Everybody knew that a great storm was coming.

Gilpatric returned to the United States and was drafted into the intelligence service. After the war, he and his wife, Louise, to whom the *Compleat Goggler* was dedicated, settled in Santa Barbara, California. His stories were still selling and he was averaging a new Glencannon book every couple of years. *Action in the North Atlantic*, a tribute to the courage of the Merchant Marine, was filmed in 1943 with Humphrey Bogart as the lead. Guy was nominated for an Oscar.

Izaak Walton had lived to be ninety, but Gilpatric was to shun that option.

In 1950 Cousteau brought the first aqualungs to the United States for them to undergo trials with the American navy. He asked to meet Gilpatric, but he was too late. Guy's beloved wife had developed breast cancer. The physician told them of the diagnosis at 2.30 one afternoon; two hours later Guy shot Louise in the temple then placed the gun in his own mouth.

He left us few mementoes, but *The Compleat Goggler* was discovered by a new generation of divers when it was republished in 1957.

And on the Côte d'Azur, Eden Roc at Cap d'Antibes, now sadly bereft of fish, will be for ever Gilpatric's, the place where it all began.

Gilpatric's sketch of his skin diving technique

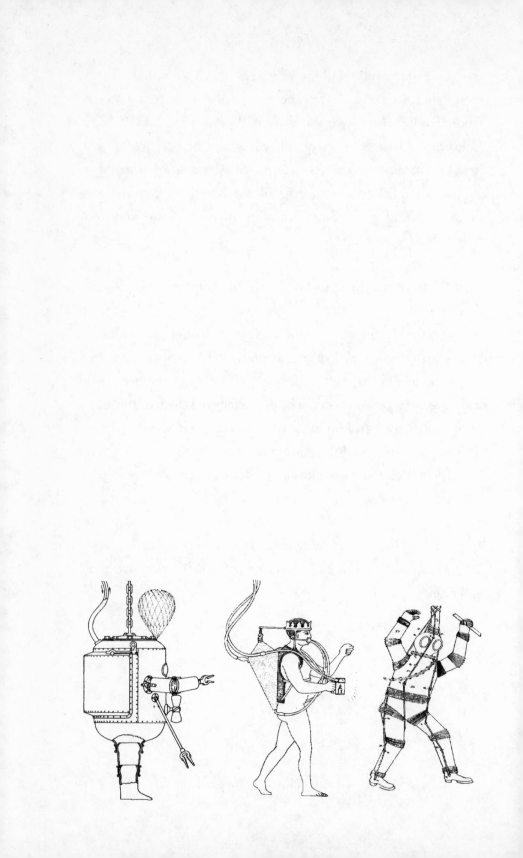

DRESS INFORMAL, BUCKETS WILL BE WORN

If you wish to stay under water for longer than a single breath allows, then you need help. Simple devices are the best, and the simplest diving equipment was the diving bell. It was lowered in to the water with its open mouth facing downwards, trapping breathable air inside. In later models the air supply could be replenished from above with the excess escaping from the bell's mouth. Its steel shell gave a spurious air of security against the crush of the water, but it was the pressure of the insubstantial air inside that kept the water at bay.

But explorers wanted to *see* the underwater world. The breakthrough was the invention of a portable diving bell like a bucket that fitted over the diver's head allowing him to breathe, and with a glass window in front enabling him to see. So a few intrepid marine biologists donned buckets and 'milk churns' and walked beneath the waves to pioneer underwater research.

Milne Edwards at his most professorial, probably late 1890s

Armed only with a pickaxe

Henri Milne Edwards 1800–1885

Naturalists have always been fascinated by the unseen underwater world, and the excitement of waiting for the dredge to spill its contents on the deck, a tumble of scallops and spider crabs and dead man's fingers. But it was a lucky dip, and not always lucky. Sometimes the bag of the dredge would be clogged with silt or bulge with stones so that the winch had to breathe hard to haul it aboard. Worst of all, these scraps gave little idea of what it was like below in that hidden world of muddy wormeries and sea-weedy meadows.

One hundred and fifty years ago diving equipment was too expensive, too difficult to use and too dangerous to tempt even the most curious naturalist beneath the waves. The first to dare was Henri Milne Edwards.

He was born in Belgium, the twenty-seventh son of an Englishman – surely some sort of record in its own right. His father was imprisoned for seven years for abetting the escape of English internees during the Napoleonic wars. The oldest brother, a physiologist, became head of the family and guided Henri away from his early interest in the arts and towards zoology.

In 1815, with Napoleon's defeat at Waterloo, the family moved to Paris, and eventually adopted French citizenship. Henri studied medicine, but soon found that he preferred crabs to the charms of cholera and croup. At the first opportunity he fled the hospital and was off to the Channel coast to study marine creatures. Three research cruises led to his classic account of the natural history of these shores.

Henri married well: to Laure Trézel, whose father was Commandant of the province of Oran. He encouraged Henri to visit the shores of North Africa in 1834, a trip that resulted in a series of works on polyps. Later General Trézel would become Minister of War.

At first Henri wrote books on surgical anatomy and pharmacological practice to supplement his income. His admission to the French Academy in 1838 was followed by appointments as head of the crustaceans, spiders and insects division in the Paris Muséum and entomologist at the Jardin des Plantes. Then came the prestigious chair of Comparative Physiology in the Faculty of Sciences at the University of Paris, where he was able to devote himself to teaching and research. But with success came sadness, for several of his children died in infancy and then his beloved wife also died after a long illness.

Henri drowned his sorrows in the sea. He had 'often had the desire to descend in a diving helmet and to be able to examine at leisure the submarine rocks inhabited by those whom I would like to make the object of my researches'. The opportunity arose when his friend, Colonel Gustave Paulin, Commandant of the Paris fire brigade, designed and built a diving helmet. The prototype was devised after eight of Paulin's men had perished in a warehouse fire. It was designed to allow fire-fighters to enter blazing cellars, 'especially those in the merchants' district, where they store alco-

Terrified fireman using Commandant Paulin's smoke hood (1837), the
precursor of Milne Edwards' diving helmet

holic liquors, sulphur, resins and other such commodities', where
the 'atmosphere is thick and caustic'. The device, for which he
won an award from the Academy of Science, was merely a hide
hood that fitted over the fireman's head and was secured by a belt
at the waist. Fresh air was pumped into the hood to allow the man
to breathe.

Although the principle was sound, the gear was clearly
unsuitable for underwater use. However, the Minister of Public
Instruction funded Paulin to develop an improved apparatus in
which Henri could descend into the sea.

In the spring of 1844 Milne Edwards together with fellow
naturalist Armand de Quatrefages, and Monsieur Blanchard, a
technician from the Muséum, set off for the clear waters of the

coast of Sicily on the first diving expedition undertaken by marine biologists. Their aim was 'to explore the coast of Sicily step by step . . . stopping wherever weed-covered rocks announced that our researches would probably be attended with success'.

Within two weeks they were anchored within the smoking shadow of Vesuvius which stood 'like some ever-present impending evil'. Active volcanoes would add to their adventures; they would see Stromboli erupting and Etna blowing perfect smoke rings. Determined not just to descend into the sea but to ascend as well, Milne Edwards and his companions climbed all three to get a closer look. On Etna, where Vulcan forged weapons for the gods, the ground rose up before them and formed a small new cone oozing lava. They climbed Stromboli at sunset and gazed down into 'the abyss kindling at our feet, whilst a magnificent jet of fire rose towards us with a noise resembling the repeated discharge of artillery . . . as if to celebrate our arrival'. They descended the mountain in the velvet blackness of a moonless night with the volcano emitting incandescent fountains at their backs and raining ash upon their heads. Quatrefages felt 'as if I were moving in a dream, in the midst of thick darkness, over ground which slid away from my feet'. And, as they left the island by boat, the waters challenged the volcano with an exhibition of phosphorescence 'kindled into a blaze of light, as if they had borrowed some of the hidden fires of Stromboli. The waves as they broke along the rocky shore encircled it with a glowing band of light, whilst every projecting cliff was circled with a wreath of fire.'

They had difficulty in finding a boat small enough to manoeuvre in shallow waters and yet sufficiently large to carry all their gear, especially the great brass double forcing pump with its balance beam, as used by all the best fire brigades of the time.

They settled for *La Santa Rosalia*, a nine-metre fishing barque named after the patron saint of Sicily. She was small enough to be rowed in calm weather and a lateen sail could be hoisted to catch the wind. The huge pump was fixed at the bow, giving such a peculiar aspect to the boat that it 'excited the strangest commentaries' in all who saw it.

There was a crew of seven, 'five of whom certainly seemed active and strong fellows' and presumably two of whom did not. The naturalists' quarters were the awning-covered well at the stern. They were supplied with three cushions 'which we dignified with the name of mattresses, together with sailors' capes which were intended to take the place of sheets and blankets'. The crew stowed themselves away as best they could, some between the benches and others on the sails and ropes like decorations on a Christmas tree.

Sometimes they would anchor during the day and row in the cool of the evening. One of the men would begin a song, and the oars 'rising and falling in cadence with the voice seemed to harmonise with the rhythm of his wild and sonorous chant. Each stroke of the oar was followed by a tremulous phosphorescence.'

The expedition proper began at Palermo, where the fleets of Carthage had once overwintered and Nelson and Lady Hamilton had overexerted themselves. In 1844 it was one of the most beautiful towns in the Mediterranean, a Moorish place of gardens and minarets. Although the mosques had now been commandeered by Christianity, their columns still bore inscriptions from the Koran. It was a place for poets. Even the expeditioners first saw it slumbering 'amid the gentle murmurs of the waves, as they flowed slowly back from its shores'.

La Santa Rosalia left Palermo heading east on a calm, clear Mediterranean morning, like that described a century later by another diver, Philippe Diolé, as 'a dream surviving the sun and languishing over a stilled sea' – he had also contracted poetry in Palermo.

But suddenly, on rounding a cape, the sea was no longer still. They found themselves running against a stiff breeze and a big swell. Milne Edwards and Quatrefages 'fell victims to all the horrors of sea-sickness and yielding to our misery, we threw ourselves upon our mattresses and were content to cast a glance from time to time at the shore which flitted past'. Their companion, Blanchard, was unaffected and 'even the most violent rolling and pitching produced no other effect upon him than to increase his appetite.'

To make matters worse, the crew, ripe with garlic and onions, worked and slept in clothes which had 'served them well for many long years [and] did not conduce to the purity of the atmosphere'. The misery was complete when armies of whirring, evil-smelling cockroaches emerged at night from every crevice in the boat and invaded their sleep.

The food didn't help. Their first meal was of rancid sausage and something that resembled very old Gruyère. 'It must be confessed,' wrote Quatrefages, 'that few persons had less claim to be regarded as a cook than this unfortunate individual', whose efforts only succeeded in 'converting the materials into a dish of hot water and sodden meat. He scarcely had managed to learn how to boil our eggs at the end of the season.'

The operation of a chain of command on the boat mystified the naturalists. When Milne Edwards asked a crewman to fill a bucket with sea water, the man walked the length of the boat and repeated the request to another sailor. He in turn informed the captain who then assembled the entire crew and announced that *Il Signor Grande* required sea water. After all this, the same crewman who had taken the empty bucket away fifteen minutes earlier returned with it full.

Whenever bad weather rocked the boat, the scientists struck out overland and rejoined the ship at its next port of call. Their treks weren't just strolls in the hills, for this was not the Mediterranean of rosemary and *Cistus* blooms, tamed by olives and vines. Sicily is nearer to Africa than to Rome. Away from the towns and the malachite sea a scrub of aloes and cacti spiked the rugged, brigand-infested country. You might see Naples and die, but probably only of cholera; Sicily offered tourists a much wider menu of dangers.

One overland trip was from Santo-Vito to Trapani, not a long journey, but 'the rough gait of the mules and the uncouth apparatus which served us in place of a saddle seemed to double the distance. The feeling of intense enjoyment with which we took possession of the not over-soft beds . . . will be readily understood by everyone who, like ourselves, had been shaken all day long on the back of a Sicilian mule or had slept for a month past between a plank and a sailor's cape.'

Carrying with them letters of introduction from high-ranking officials, they found that 'despotism . . . is a very convenient institution for those whom it favours; in Sicily, where officials are the living impersonations of the law, our letters of recommendation were all-potent in placing us above ordinary regulations.' The locals also provided them with lodgings, all of which left something to be desired and some, *everything* to be desired. At Torre dell' Isola they stayed in what had once been the residence of the Counts of Capaci. They were given rooms 'in which everything betokened the most complete neglect . . . The ancient frescos . . . had long since crumbled into dust. The lofty windows with their rotten frames seemed as if they would break into fragments in our hands when we tried to open them. Time had coated the few panes that still remained with so thick a layer of dust, that

they had lost all transparency. There was nowhere a vestige of furniture.' At Catellamare their rooms had first to be cleared of a pile
of rotting onions.

Throughout western Sicily there 'remained mournful
vestiges of former splendour which had long since given place to
misery. Grass grew abundantly in the straight streets; on every side
palaces were in ruins, scarcely able to afford shelter to the few
beggars who had appropriated them.'

The boat then arrived off the little-visited islands of
Favignana where the public clock was a man with a sand hourglass
who struck the hours on a bell. Their arrival produced the same
effect as 'throwing a stone into an ant-hill'. Nothing was too
much trouble for the locals; they even demolished a wall to allow
access to the shore, although when they realised that their reward
would be in compliments rather than cash, their efforts waned
considerably.

The local limestone shores had the richest fauna the
naturalists had ever seen: 'A cubic foot of this stone would afford
materials for an entire collection . . . no place could be better
adapted for zoological investigations.'

The biologists were also in time to see *la mattanza* (the
slaughter), an annual massed tuna hunt. 'By the break of day, as
far as the eye could reach, the sea seemed covered with . . . a hundred broad lateen sails.' The huge fish were guided through a
series of nets, with 'doors' closing behind them, each 'room'
smaller than the previous one: *il salone, il salottino, la sala da pranzo*
(the dining room), until they were trapped in the final *camera della
morte* (chamber of death). For several hours the bronzed, half-
naked fishermen stabbed and gaffed the thrashing fish, turning the
sea crimson. 'All eyes are sparkling,' wrote Quatrefages:

all lips are uttering cries of triumph . . . [But
the spectacle] left us melancholy and
discontented, for we had been most painfully
affected by the exhibition of such wholesale
butchery . . . It seemed to us impossible to
avoid feeling the deepest emotion . . . in
observing the mute anguish in which the
convulsive movements of the victims were the
only indications of the agony which was so
wantonly inflicted upon them. It was quite
different for the sailors, who were perfectly
radiant with delight.

A 'charming group of ladies' had come from Palermo to witness
the two hours of carnage.

The annual ritual continues to this day, but whereas in the
1840s it netted up to ten thousand tuna, it now yields only a few
hundred. Still, the guide book assures us, the tourists enjoy it.

On the Atlantic coast the retreating tide uncovered great
fields of seaweed and a menagerie of scuttling and slithering life,
but here in the Mediterranean, where the tidal range was only a
metre, most of the animals were under water and out of reach.
Quatrefages gazed longingly over the side of the boat:

We stared down at the hills, valleys and plains
passing before our eyes . . . rocky precipices
that plunged down for perhaps a hundred feet
into the depths, and everywhere the
undulations . . . stood out with such
astonishing clarity that we began to lose a
sense of reality. . . We seemed to be suspended

in mid-air, or rather to be in the middle of one
of those dreams all men have from time to
time, that feeling of gliding through the air and
looking down at the thousand and one features
of the landscape beneath. But beings with
strange shapes peopled that underwater
landscape . . .

Only diving gear could give them access to this mysterious
world. According to Milne Edwards, the equipment was a large,
open-bottomed 'metallic reservoir in the form of a helmet, com-
municating by means of long flexible tube, with a pump through
which air could be forced. Covered with this helmet, which had a
glass visor, and the lower part of which was fitted with a cushion
placed around the neck, I allowed myself the help of lead sandals
as a counterpoise to the mass of air I needed to carry with me to
the depths.' There was also a small tap on the front beneath the
visor so that excess air could be expelled. I doubt that too much
air was ever a problem; too much water was. The helmet had to
kept upright. If the diver leaned forward, the sea rushed in and
drowning became a distinct possibility.

Henri admitted that 'the diving helmet, owing to its volume
and weight, was not easy to use.' Worst of all, I imagine, were the
long stirrups that stretched from his feet to the helmet to keep it
in place.

Thus encumbered, the learned professor descended into the
sea for the first time. With Lipari and Vulcano brooding on the
horizon, he plummeted into Milazzo harbour, where consul
Duilius had defeated the Carthaginian fleet over two thousand
years before.

On the boat above, the crew laboured over the great rocking

arms of the pump and 'the air thus injected promptly arrived down to me and then escaped via the open spaces between the neck and the lower edge of the helmet, serving not only to supply my respiration but also to prevent the water rising to the level of my mouth, which would have suffocated me.'

Armed only with a pickaxe, Milne Edwards was determined 'to pursue marine creatures into their most hidden retreats'. He ambled below 'in the enjoyment of perfect liberty of action', stopping only to examine 'the fissures of the submarine rocks which thronged with molluscs, worms and zoophytes . . . I could see everything around me perfectly, and it was only muscular fatigue which prevented me from strolling around on the sea bed as one does in the ordinary way on the shore.'

He stayed below for half an hour at a depth of thirteen feet, with Quatrefages clutching the life-line and nervously peering over the side. 'God knows with what anxiety I watched its faintest motion. The slightest mistake might have proved fatal to Milne Edwards. It certainly requires an amount of zeal very uncommon among naturalists of our day to risk so perilous an undertaking.'

The safest feature of the open diving helmet was that if anything went wrong the diver could duck out from beneath, shed the helmet and swim up to the surface, but not of course if he was wearing lead sandals. Henri had taken the precaution of securing a line from his harness over the ship's yardarm so that, when he signalled by tugging it, he could be hauled up to safety. That at least was the theory, but it was the safety rope that almost caused an emergency. One day the sea got up whilst he was below and he had to be retrieved in a hurry. Unfortunately, Henri was forty-four years old and rather plump. When he was halfway up, the yardarm cracked, he plummeted back to the bottom and had to be heaved up hand over hand. Another time he accidentally tugged on the line and was surprised when hauled to the surface to find the crew leaping into the water to save him. In the excitement one of the sailors had forgotten he couldn't swim and he had to be rescued before he drowned. However, it had taken over five minutes to drag Milne Edwards to the surface — ample time in which to asphyxiate had he really been in difficulties.

Henri dived daily, penetrating deeper and staying longer. 'We have seen him, at a depth of upwards of twenty-five feet below the surface of the water, for more than three-quarters of an hour with a pickaxe to detach some of those large panopeas [clams].' Milne Edwards was confident that 'it would have been simple to descend to much greater depths had not the inadequacy of the life-saving facilities on the fishing boat made me think that it would have been imprudent to try.'

Some of the creatures he observed in the shallows had never been seen alive before, including sea slugs with 'a spangled veil of finest gauze stretched over the head of these lovely creatures'. He was the first marine biologist to describe living subtidal communities and 'every time he came up from the bottom his specimen box was full with a rich harvest'.

The expedition was a success. They returned with filled notebooks and crates of specimens. Blanchard found insects swarming over the fields and gathered over two thousand species, of which three hundred were new to science. Quatrefages was charged with collecting reptiles for 'the curious menagerie which had been opened at the Jardin des Plantes', but found time to pursue his studies on shellfish and bisexual worms. All this stimulated him to consider 'that mysterious force which animates the alga and the oak, the infusorian and the elephant, [which] becomes manifest to us as a universal cause, whose intimate nature eludes our search . . .'

Milne Edwards' objective was to study the nervous and blood circulation systems of various marine animals and collect an immense number of eggs in order to follow their development. He cultured them in small natural basins into which the sea water seeped. Marine animals were of special interest as their tiny larvae bore no resemblance to the adults they would become. Indeed, most larvae of marine invertebrates had been classified as species in their own right. He was the first to follow their startling metamorphoses into the adult.

Milne Edwards was impressed with his first glimpses of the underwater world, but he never dived again. On his return to Paris he suffered intermittently from ill-health and resumed his laboratory work. He pioneered studies of the physiology of invertebrates and in developmental biology.

His life was typically that of the engrossed academic, but there were exciting interludes. During the siege of Paris in 1870 he braved the bombardment to save precious specimens in the Jardin des Plantes, some of which had been collected on his expedition to Sicily.

He was not the only biologist in the family. His older brother, William-Frédéric, caused a sensation with his book on the physiological characteristics of different races of men, and founded the study of ethnology in France. Perhaps Henri's greatest pleasure was that his son, Alphonse, also became a zoologist and in his turn led scientific cruises to investigate the deep-water fauna of the Atlantic and the Mediterranean.

Milne Edwards wrote weighty tomes on the biology of corals and molluscs and mammals. A comparative anatomy of humans and other animals ran to fourteen volumes. His natural history of the Crustacea, although only a three-volume effort, was a landmark study in which he brought order to the group, describing hundreds of new species. Although it failed to make the bestseller list, his work was known to Jules Verne. In *Twenty Thousand Leagues Under the Sea*, Professor Aronnax, the captive passenger on the submarine *Nautilus*, was Professor of Natural History at the Paris Muséum and clearly based on Milne Edwards. He even refers to 'Milne Edwards, my worthy master'. That is closer to immortality than most scientists achieve.

In an age where professional biologists were content to pore over dried plants and pickled cadavers, Milne Edwards was one of the first to realise what now seems obvious; to understand how animals function you must study *live* specimens – 'My opinion as to the inadequacy of research made on animals preserved in alcohol was further confirmed. The observation of living animals allows you to recognise the cause of errors . . . and to correct them.'

He was a true naturalist who had endured danger and discomfort to see how organisms really lived. Where he had led under water, others would follow.

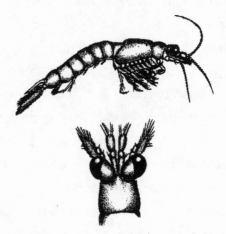

Acanthomysis longicornis (The long-horned thorny ghost shrimp). One of the many species first described and named by Milne Edwards

SEA

Roy Miner and his lamp both scrutinising a specimen under his microscope,
around 1930
(*Detail from photograph, courtesy of Library Services, American Museum of Natural History*)

The very
nearly man

Roy Waldo Miner 1875–1955

Roy Miner, from Massachusetts, was a studious and diligent pupil and from the outset everyone knew that he would go far, but not perhaps very far. He graduated from Williams College in 1897 and entered the General Theological Seminary in New York. Although he was never to become a cleric, he would henceforth adopt the prose of the pulpit and marshal homilies to describe the antics of the creatures he eventually came to study.

Roy became a schoolteacher, of Latin and biology, and then an associate headmaster. He married in 1903 and the arrival of three children would have strained his income, had he not joined the staff of the American Museum of Natural History in New York as assistant curator of invertebrate zoology. He was to work there for the next thirty-eight years.

It was one of the greatest museums in the world, with limitless ambition and inexhaustible benefactors. The complex of fifteen buildings flanking Central Park was a twenty-three acre maze of great halls, laboratories and corridors. In 1938 its collections were conservatively valued at $30 million. They included 3,000 meteorites, 800,000 birds, more than a million shells and 12 million insects. It also possessed J. P. Morgan's gem collection from Tiffany's and the pelt of a St Bernard dog that had once had a flair for playing dominoes.

Miner's task was to design new exhibits, so he constructed simulations of the tide pools and the wharf pilings of the New England coast. These were not aquaria, but full-sized tableaux inhabited by model sea stars, butterfish, and worms named after goddesses and nymphs: *Aphrodite, Lycidice, Amphitrite* . . .

Miner was a meticulous man. The models had to be accurate and how better to ensure this than to visit the shore and observe the creatures at first hand. He was enthralled. 'Suddenly,' he writes, 'the weed at the left is parted and out stalks a large "buckie", or furbelowed whelk, like a hero of a play stepping forth from the wings of a theatre.' Everywhere there was a secret beauty. The tentacled rosettes of tubeworms entranced him.

> As we watch, a beautiful flower-like head emerges from a tube opening and unfolds a circlet of delicate fern-shaped plumes . . . Heads now appear from tube after tube, until the whole surface of the ledge blossoms with animal flowers in every shade of gorgeous color. Some . . . patriotically adorned with red, white and blue stripes . . . Accidentally, we pass a hand . . . casting a shadow over the pulsating garden. Within the twinkling of an eye, every circlet closes and pops back into its tube . . . their fragile beauty is far removed from the unaesthetic ugliness of their relative, the earthworm.

Using a glass-bottomed 'waterglass' he viewed the life on the rotting piles of an abandoned wharf. 'The whole pile is a gorgeous sea garden, completely covered with gaily colored and luxuriant growths as far down as our vision can penetrate through the dusk of the green sea water.' The underwater world beckoned him.

He also began to design exhibits of tropical creatures, and to do so properly he would first have to inspect the tropics. Between 1911 and 1915 he visited Puerto Rico and four archipelagos in the Caribbean to collect specimens. Having now got a feeling for the tropics, he conceived the project that was to consume over thirteen years of his life. He would build in the museum a full-sized replica of a coral reef – a real reef. So in 1923 he set off for the Bahamas to search for the perfect reef and found it off the island of Andros. It was 'massive, wild and grotesquely beautiful'.

It was the era of expeditions and of great discoveries. The Museum of Natural History sent out a dozen expeditions a year; forty men and a hundred and fifty camels crossed the Gobi Desert to return with a fossil mastodon, and the first placental mammal from the age of the dinosaurs, together with seventy dinosaur eggs. One of Miner's colleagues had discovered *Tyrannosaurus rex*.

The museum's curators were stout fellows in those days. One was bitten by vipers, another pinned to the ground by the tusks of an enraged elephant, a third throttled a leopard with his bare hands before it could rip him apart. And poor Akeley died of fever in the Congo before his African exhibit was finished.

Miner was tailored from less promising material. In his entry in *Who's Who*, he stresses 'Republican and Episcopalian', then, as an afterthought, 'member of the explorers' club of Williams College', the institution he had left over thirty years before.

In 1923 Miner mounted his first major expedition. He took with him artists and modellers and photographers to record the inhabitants of the reef. The film maker, Ernest Williamson, came too, bringing his fantastic underwater tube from which a metal sphere big enough to take two or three observers dangled beneath the waves. 'I shall never forget my first view of the barrier reef seen through the window of the tube,' Miner wrote. 'Great trees of reef-forming coral . . . a veritable stone forest with closely interlacing branches, a marble jungle which melted into the pearly haze . . .' The artists sat in the sphere sketching whilst a crew on a barge above moved the sphere along the reef. A swell set the sphere rising and falling and the tube swinging like a pendulum. After the sphere crashed against the reef its use was restricted to calm days. Even so, the artists completed over sixty watercolour sketches.

The biggest asset was Williamson's barge, the *Jules Verne*. The ten-ton chain hoist that lowered and raised the tube could be used to haul up big specimens. A sling was secured around the coral, the chain pulled taut and then the next wave jerked loose a two-ton specimen. A big steel-fingered grab, like those tiny funfair cranes that always drop the prize just before you get it to the chute, was used to break off smaller corals.

Miner had also taken two Miller-Dunn open-bottomed diving helmets – not very different from that worn by Milne Edwards. One artist sat twenty-five feet down in a helmet and with easel and palette, painted in oils on canvas fixed to a sheet of glass. His wooden-handled brushes floated away and had to be recovered from the surface so often that eventually he resorted to a palette knife.

Roy Miner also used the sixty-five-pound helmet to venture beneath the sea for the first time and stroll between the corridors of coral:

I swallowed once to relieve the increasing pressure on my eardrums, and at the twenty-second rung stepped off the ladder on to the white sand of the sea bottom. A huge black sting ray rose from almost under my feet and swam slowly off with graceful undulations. I had missed him by inches!

My air hose floated coiling to the surface, while clouds of silvery bubbles, released momentarily from my shoulders, rose in expanding clouds. A disturbance in the water at the summit of the ladder attracted my attention. A pair of legs appeared weirdly on the rungs. The body was not yet visible, being concealed by the liquid mirror of the water surface. This . . . reflected an inverted image of the legs, giving the odd effect of a St Andrew's cross.

Cliffs of living coral overhung me . . . These flanked deep, mysterious caverns, within whose depths I could perceive wavering light beams dancing down from concealed openings, in shafts of weird, luminous blue.

A trigger fish swam right up to the helmet's visor to peer in, moving its pursed mouth as if it were trying to kiss him. His wife also donned a helmet and descended, not to profer a clanking kiss, but to mesmerise him with the image of a mermaid with a hob-goblin's head.

He had taken three hand-cranked movie cameras in

watertight boxes. These fixed-focus cameras were frustrating to use. 'It was tantalising to see beautiful queen triggers and grotesque trumpet fishes come into plain view at a distance of twenty-five feet, when we had arranged our focus at ten feet.'

Miner in 1932, 25 feet down with camera set up to just miss taking a photograph of an octopus

Setting up was also laborious as a tripod had to be 'slowly and painfully' erected on the sea floor. Then the camera was lowered from the boat, carried over to the tripod and slotted into position. 'Unfortunately, by this time the parrot fishes had disappeared.' This happened time after time. 'The bulb-shaped body and baleful eyes of an octopus glided forward until the whole creature oozed over the edge of the coral shelf . . . Lifting the heavy box to the tripod top, I looked around for the octopus, hoping to get a picture of it, but it had disappeared.'

Although they took colour pictures under water, it was essential for the artists on the surface to have live specimens to paint. For small creatures they found they could collect all they wanted by breaking off the coral clusters, bringing them up to the

boat and dousing them up and down in a tub of water. For big-
ger fish Miner resorted to the 'bang-bang', a ten-foot bamboo
pole with two dynamite caps on the end. An insulated waterproof
cable rose from the pole to a dory on the surface. In the boat sat
a sailor with the switchbox between his legs. The diver below
swung the pole close to a victim, signalled to the surface and the
sailor set off the charge, stunning both fish and diver. A local
skin-diver then swam down, scooped up the fish in a net and
delivered it for the artist to sketch before its colours faded. A
mould was then made of the fish so that later it could be cast in
wax and shaped into a lifelike pose while the wax was still warm.

The artificial reef in the museum was not going to be fabricated in plaster or wax; it was to be constructed of real coral.
'Some corals break at a touch,' he admitted, 'others resist the
whack of a hammer.' Crowbars were used to prise off great lumps
of the reef that were then left on the shore and periodically wetted
so that the living tissue decayed away leaving the bleached limestone bones of the coral. Back in New York these would be
coated with beeswax to simulate their living tissue, and painted in
their original hues. Thirty-one cases of coral were packed in ten
boatloads of sponge clippings and shipped back to the USA.

In one area, 'the bottom was carpeted over extended areas
with the most beautiful corals I have ever seen, of an almost
inconceivable delicacy and fragility.' One of the locals 'dived
indefatigably for the beautiful specimens and we brought back an
overflowing boatload.'

They discovered a remarkable coral growth twelve feet tall,
like an immense rosette, its broad fronds arranged spirally in ever
diminishing tiers. 'You want him?' asked the diver. 'Yes, of course
I do,' Miner admitted. They used a block and tackle and a hoist
to haul it aboard and later found it weighed 900 pounds. The

largest single specimen they collected weighed two tons. This expedition alone collected forty tons of coral. It can take a reef a hundred years to restore a day's damage, but if Miner had any doubts about the destruction, he never voiced them.

When it was too rough to dive they demolished one of the low rocky cays and, by means of hammer and hatchet, hacked off huge fragments of the eroded honeycomb rock. They obtained more than a ton of this rock and shipped it off to the museum.

There would be five expeditions to the Bahamas between 1923 and 1933 to collect more specimens of corals, fish and sea fans and to verify that the painted corals were the same colour as the live specimens. The museum decided it would also like a tableau of a pearl-diving scene so off he went to Tongareva in the South Pacific, diving five times a day a couple of bays along from where two local boys were being eaten by sharks. He collected 'ten and a half more tons of beautiful corals, upwards of 100 pearl shells, about the same number of tridacnas [giant clams] and several thousand specimens of invertebrates.'

The museum did nothing by halves. It boasted the largest meteorite ever found, the biggest collection of dinosaur skeletons and a herd of seven stuffed elephants. Even the model of a blue-bottle was forty times larger than life. Clearly the reef exhibit would have to be impressive, and it was.

It occupied two levels. From a balcony, as if leaning over a ship's rail, you could view the reef from above the 'water's' surface of rippled glass. In the foreground were the honeycomb rocks and windswept palms of Goat Cay and beyond the Andros reef lay the Tongue of Ocean painted on a huge, domed cyclorama.

Visitors then descended as a diver might to the level of the sea floor below, where the mighty reef occupied an area of almost 8,000 square feet and rose to a height of seventeen feet. Seven tons of steel scaffolding supported forty tons of big corals, to which thousands of smaller ones and hundreds of sea fans had been fixed. Painted glass plates eleven feet tall were inserted for middle-ground effects. Over five hundred model fish were suspended 'in mid-water'. It was monumental.

The public were amazed, but Roy Miner surely knew that the magic of a real reef lay in movement: the rippling sun flecks on the white sand, the lazy sway of seaweed, fish busily browsing, fluttering and fleeing, the lightning chase of predators and prey. The great static reef display that he had so meticulously built was opened in 1935 and demolished in the early 1960s to make way for the new Great Hall of Ocean Life.

Miner received a doctorate in philosophy from Columbia University in 1923 and an honorary degree from his Alma Mater a year later. He became president of the New York Academy of Science and editor of its journal, but he was never a renowned academic. His great work was to be a manual of the seashore creatures of the Atlantic coast of the USA, but it took too long to produce. Publication was 'imminent' in 1935 although it did not appear until 1950, by which time the names of many of the animals had changed.

He devoted his life to popularising marine biology, writing articles for magazines such as the *National Geographic*. Sometimes he captured the essence of an underwater creature: 'A file fish, with a quadrangular body, foolish shape . . . swam past like a gaily colored impossibility . . . Wrasses of every sort, brilliant in rose, purple, green, blue and gold, darted about in all directions. The water around us was full of broken rainbows.'

He also had a flair for conveying the obvious: 'The staghorn coral builds loosely branching many-tined skeletons reminding one of the antlers of a stag, from which its name is derived. The

. . . great elkhorn forms gigantic growths with branches like beams, expanding into broad, palmate tips, reminding one of the antlers of an elk.'

Miner almost encountering a shark

The general public was eager to be thrilled by undersea adventures – if only he'd had some. His exploits were so nearly exciting, but not quite. He was stung by a Portuguese man-of-war and he shouted at a shark, but that was about it. 'Once a bar-racuda, more dreaded than sharks, swam over my head while I was engaged with the camera; but I didn't know it till I came to the surface and Captain Joe told me about it.' He became the master of anti-climax:

The famous palolo worm was due to swarm
. . . on two days of the year . . . the long,
slender hinder portion of the worm . . .
becomes detached. These segments then swim
out in countless numbers at the surface of the
water to mate, and a myriad are caught as food
by the natives . . . Rising before dawn on the
great day, they set forth in canoes and with
hand nets and baskets scoop up whole boat
loads of the teeming worms . . . On this
occasion the islanders were disappointed,
however, as the swarming did not take place.

Roy Miner was the adventurer who almost had an adventure, but he had missed the boat; he had even misnamed the boat. Whereas other more glamorous explorers would one day voyage on the *Calypso* and the *Xarifa*, he went to sea on the 'gasoline yacht, *Standard J*'.

He so nearly became famous, but never did. Celebrity awaited a contemporary who did much the same things, but described them so much better and brought the underwater world alive. His name was William Beebe.

A beknighted William Beebe about to joust with sea creatures in the
'kingdom of the helmet', 1925 (© *W. Beebe*)

The delights of dangling

Charles William Beebe 1877–1962

William Beebe sprang from an English family that had inhabited the north-eastern seaboard of the United States since 1650. Young Will was nurtured on history and the adventure stories of G. A. Henty and Jules Verne, but his real-life adventures were confined to studying birds and insects in the fields of New Jersey. He was an only child and his mother, Henrietta, had great expectations of him. Once he had shown an interest in natural history she thrust him to the attention of leading zoologists. It was fortunate that he didn't object, and a zoologist he was going to be.

He was soon off to Columbia University, but in 1899 the recently founded New York Zoological Society required an assistant curator of birds at the Bronx zoo. So young Will abandoned his studies and took the job. He never did get his degree, although he later angered the university authorities by claiming he had.

He was responsible for the construction of the largest aviary in the world ('Beebe's big bird house'), in which bird behaviour could be studied in relatively natural conditions. He was often seen peddling swiftly around the zoo on his bicycle importuning startled visitors to hurry along to his latest exhibit.

Beebe soon tired of life at the zoo and at the age of twenty-
six he and his new wife, Mary, visited Mexico. It was the first of
sixty expeditions to the jungles and tropical islands of the world
that he would mount for the Zoological Society. As director of
the Society's Department of Tropical Research, he devoted eight
years to studying a quarter square mile of jungle in British Guiana.

From the beginning he wrote of his adventures, and wrote
well. Here he describes nightfall in the Himalayas:

> Without warning, the sun dropped behind a
> distant ridge. It was as if someone had turned
> out some enormous lamp. Luminous clouds
> appeared in the air that before had been so
> clear, and the first whisper of the cold night
> wind echoed softly in the crags. The insects
> vanished, and one by one the icicles and
> rivulets were silenced at the touch of the
> coming twilight. From a high ravine came the
> plaintive call of a white-capped redstart, and a
> gray fox barked from somewhere afar off.
> Then, in the rich afterglow reflected from the
> mountains of snow, seven birds appeared over
> the crest of the ridge. They came slowly, one
> after the other, and I knew them at once for
> the blood pheasants I had come so far to find.

He had a five-year leave of absence to hunt down the pheasants of the world. With Mary he trudged the Himalayas, tasted
the choleral delights of Malaya, took the train to Mandalay and a
mule train across into China. They sampanned down the
Yangtze, then crossed the black steppes of Mongolia on camels.

They were dogged by 'terrific snow and wind storms and the prevalence of plague'. That was the least of it. William shot dead a threatening tribesman, a bearer shoved him out of the path of a leaping tiger, and their Chinese cook turned out to have been a multiple poisoner. There was also a skirmish from which his tracker returned with eight fresh human heads dangling from his belt, one better than the tailor who killed 'seven at one blow'. Beebe fell down through a thicket and grasped a passing branch that turned out to be a king cobra. He recounted these tales with admirable understatement; after all, the cobra is nowhere near as poisonous as the fer-de-lance – which he would encounter later in the week.

Mary seemed to endure and enjoy these hardships, but within a year of their return she had filed for divorce on the grounds of 'cruelty and indifference'. There were claims of miserliness yet reckless spending, domestic silence but public rows. He was said to have threatened suicide by flinging himself into a river, thrusting a revolver into his mouth and slashing his throat with a razor. NATURALIST WAS CRUEL, proclaimed the front page of the *New York Times*. The divorce was uncontested.

He then embarked on more expeditions accompanied by a devoted band of female assistants given such improbable titles as 'historian and technicist', and 'assistant in fish problems'.

Beebe was a thin, active man who seemed to have been balding from birth. His high-domed head and quizzical eyes gave him the look of an alert egg. He was an indifferently upholstered six-footer, but looked much taller, as if he'd been drawn out on the rack. As a youth he had won a medal at pole-vaulting, and there was some debate as to where William ended and the pole began.

His passion was taxonomy, the classification and naming of

living things. At first he studied birds, but as a child he had clutched a rock so that he could sink into the shallows to observe sea anemones; now it was his interest in fish – the birds of the sea – that tempted him again beneath the waves.

In 1925 he cruised to the Galápagos islands. *En route* he searched for the mighty Humboldt current but failed to find it. Its absence was 'inexplicable', and would not be explained for many years until it was realised that the great currents of the Pacific Ocean periodically change route and play havoc with the climate of the Pacific rim. It was christened the El Niño phenomenon.

Before setting off, Beebe had bought a large copper helmet with two oblique windows at the front, and a rubber garden hose to carry air from a small car tyre hand pump to the helmet. He was a little concerned for 'the paraphernalia accompanying it were so simple that I doubted its efficiency.' He was pleasantly surprised when he made his first dives into what he called 'the kingdom of the helmet', and discovered 'the delights of dangling'. He wore only the helmet, rubber-soled shoes, and, not wishing to attract onlookers, a bathing suit

'The first time I climbed down my submerged ladder,' he wrote:

> I knew that I had added thousands upon thousands of miles to my possible joy of earthly life . . . From the moment one is submerged, the reality of the absolute apartness of this place is apparent. In the air one weighs thirteen stone or so – here one can leap twelve feet, or lift oneself with a crook of a finger. A fall from a cliff is only a gentle drifting downward, and one's whole activity

> . . . the exquisite grace of a slow-motion
> picture . . . Here miracles become marvels, and
> marvels recurring wonders.

According to Beebe there were only two possibilities if
someone ventured under water: 'If one dives and returns to the
surface inarticulate with amazement . . . then he deserves to go
again and again. If he is unmoved or disappointed, then there
remains for him on earth only a longer or shorter period of waiting for death; there can be little worth while left in life for him.'

Beebe dismissed the dangerous creatures of the deep: 'Giant
octopuses or barracudas or sharks – don't give them a thought',
but he was lucky that some of his encounters turned out so well.
He was reaching to net a fish under water when, 'out of this cloud
of roiled water at my elbow, rose the head and neck of one of the
largest green morays I have ever seen, also reaching for my fish . . .
I kicked with all my might. It was spontaneous resentment at the
danger of losing my specimen, and I gave no thought to the possible result.' Luckily, the eight-foot tine-toothed eel retreated in
surprise. That same day, whilst tempting fish with a baited pole,

> a great grey crescent shoved in beside me . . .
> it was the snout of a five-foot shark, which had
> materialised from nowhere . . . The shark
> pushed ahead directly across my hand, and I
> saw that my puffer [fish] had slipped from the
> net, and that the slanting eyes of the shark had
> perceived it. It was attempting to work itself
> past and against my leaning body. This was
> too much; I shifted my grip on the net and
> stabbed down with the handle, with all my

force, directly on the rounded snout. A terrific
swirl of water . . . the shark backed out and
undulated over my head . . . I recaught the
puffer.

Pressure was of greater concern to him. 'Forty feet is a good
limit to set,' he cautioned and warned that, if 'already eight or ten
fathoms down, don't let any alluring shell or coral lure you
deeper.' He never ventured below sixty feet: 'It would be exceedingly unwise to go much farther, for the weight of the water had
already increased the pressure on my eardrums and every portion
of my body to almost forty-five pounds per square inch. At
double the depth I had reached I would probably become insens-
ible and unable to ascend.'

Beebe, like all divers, soon became cluttered with gear. For
making notes while sitting on a comfortable block of coral, he
used a zinc sheet or a pad of waterproof paper, but ensured his
pencil was securely bound and tethered, 'for otherwise the wood
. . . will float to the surface while the core of lead sinks to the
bottom'. Pencils have come a long way since the 1920s.

He took photographs and movies under water but advised
the more traditionally minded who wished to paint, 'Weight your
easel with lead, waterproof your canvas . . . and sit down with your
palette of oils.' Although he admits, 'You will have to brush away
small fish from time to time . . . and your palette will sometimes
be covered with a hungry school of inchlings.'

'If your tastes incline to sport, invent submarine slingshots
and crossbows and shoot what particular fish you wish with
barbed arrows of brass wire. I now use dynamite caps on the end
of a weighted fish pole, but slingshots are safer for the beginner.'
He carried a large wad of cotton wool down with him to indulge

in his 'favorite underwater sport of sponge stuffing', bunging up the creature's 'mouths'.

Smashing open coral attracted fish for him to study. 'A desert of animal life,' he boasted, 'can be converted into a populated oasis by a few strokes of a crowbar.' Bait was useful too. 'A sight I shall not forget is that of a dead horse which we tied to the western buoy, and at sunset Almost Island was alive with sharks.'

Beebe hands up his catch, a fat sea cucumber plucked from the sea floor, about 1930 (*W. Beebe*)

His main aim was to collect and identify as many creatures as possible. He had succumbed to the lure of the list. On seeing a strange bird he admits: 'As I didn't recognise it, I shot it.' Whilst game fishing in the Galápagos, he observes that 'fish savagery is always a striking feature of sea-fishing . . . The moment either one seems to be in trouble or incapacitated he immediately becomes a victim. The attack seems more savage than the kill of the jungle.' So he joined in the spirit of the thing. 'A seven-foot shark took all of an hour to subdue, even with the help of many shots from a Luger and several charges from a shotgun at short range.' He also 'caught' flying fish from the prow of a speeding launch with a shotgun, 'a most exciting and difficult sport'.

On an expedition to Baja California he encountered a whale shark, the biggest fish in the sea, but a harmless plankton sifter. The crew attached an oil drum float to a big harpoon:

> When we came alongside the fish . . . we waited until she was almost awash, then both men made a beautiful pole-vaulting dive, with the harpoon between them. They struck hard and then leaped into the air and let their whole weight bear down, driving the harpoon home. At that same moment I fired a revolver straight into the creature's head, making at least two direct hits. The drum was thrown overboard and vanished.
>
> After fifteen minutes . . . there three hundred yards away was the float. We found it completely crumpled in the middle like a huge hour-glass, evidence of the pressure at the great depth to which it must have been dragged . . . and for the next hour had the excitement of our lives.
>
> Twice we returned to the yacht for additional harpoons, but in spite of the greatest efforts the instruments bent as if they had struck steel . . . Finally we tightened the noose around the drum . . . it was made fast. But the moment he felt the pull of the yacht he tore out the harpoon as if it had been a pin, and was off.

The US Marine Corps trained Beebe to deploy dynamite:

> We set off two sticks of dynamite with the
> usual excellent results . . . I saw an astonishing
> sight . . . the explosion had occurred in the
> midst of a rain of fleeing silversides . . . and the
> reef floor looked like tinsel on a Christmas
> tree.

You might think that marine creatures would have hidden whenever he appeared, but unsuspecting animals 'from shrimps to sharks accepted me as something new but harmless which the waves had washed in.'

'A wise diver will refrain from written descriptions of his experiences,' he advised. But he never refrained.

'If you wish to make a garden,' he added for the conservation-minded, 'choose some . . . grotto and with a hatchet chop and pry off coral boulders with waving purple sea-plumes, golden sea-fans and great parti-coloured anemones. Wedge these into crevices . . . finally as a border to your marine plantation, collect a score of small, round brain corals . . .'

Beebe had a gift for describing the behaviour of the organisms he didn't manage to kill: fish were 'nomads, shovellers, surfers, percolators, squatters or villagers' and when shoaling they became 'a maze of fluttering, golden flags . . . furling and unfurling'. The fate of most sea creatures is to be eaten unless they are lucky or agile or well protected. Distasteful beasts usually advertise the fact and 'not a moment passes but somewhere a color secret is exploded, an inedible bluff called'.

Animals were to him characters in a drama: albatrosses skimming the waves 'possess all the secrets of white shadows', the 'evil-mouthed' moray eels have 'a pessimistic viciousness', whereas sea-horses are 'motherly knights in armour'. Barracudas sometimes adopt 'a supercilious expression' and sharks are 'chinless cowards'. His favourites were perhaps the gobies, who 'of all fish, give the impression of being less completely bound up in fishiness'.

He also caught the grace and exuberance of the marine mammals:

> At this moment of dawn-grey light I forgot the clouds for a mighty school of dolphins, rolling so lazily, breathing so leisurely, that they must all have been sound asleep. Like the shaft of an engine barely turning over the propellers, they came up, curved and dived with a single magnificent motion. All in the same instant they caught the sound of the yacht . . . and two hundred leaps came as one . . . like the fragments of a bomb they churned off and bounded high in the air . . . They passed just ahead, still leaping skyward, flippers spread, slapping back with cracks like rifle shots.

Beebe was a born publicist and a genius at persuading the rich to finance his expeditions. On the very day he returned from a trip to the Galápagos Islands he was introduced to a newly elected member of the management board of the New York Zoological Society. 'You seem tremendously interested in the Galápagos,' said the trustee. 'If you ever want to go back there, I will furnish the steamer if you can get someone else to provide the coal.' He did, and the next expedition set sail within a year. Years later he confessed, 'I wanted to make one brief sea venture, then one millionaire gave me a yacht, another millionaire gave me a yacht, and the Governor of Bermuda gave me an island. I spent ten years under water.'

Whilst they were in the Galápagos Islands two new volcanoes erupted and were promptly named in honour of his sponsors. Beebe and an assistant set off across the jagged lava in the baking sun to observe the birth of a volcano. Exhaustion had set in even before they came to the smouldering crater. They avoided the sulphurous vapours only to be overcome by more deadly, invisible fumes. Nauseous and blinded, they staggered out of the crater and headed back, taking whichever route seemed least terrible. Their water was gone long before they arrived back, exhausted and unable to speak. They had been away for five hours.

Just offshore the sea temperature beside the ship was ninety-nine degrees. Beebe described the tragic fate of a sea lion that ventured too near to the molten streams hissing into the sea: 'Five times he sprang, arching over eight to ten feet clear of the seething water and in blind agony headed straight for the scarlet delta of the lava . . . straight to death.' The next day they steamed away from the Galápagos, but the ship's steering failed and the wooden vessel drifted helplessly. Had it failed a day earlier they might have shared the sea lion's fate.

Beebe felt an affinity for the sea and captured its moods. Far from shore one day in a small boat, he cut the motor and drifted on the big, smooth swell in silence, sliding into 'a hollow of ocean walled with water for yards above our heads, or balanced, still in a breathless hush, poised on a motionless swell high in the air . . . Then gently again down, down, down.'

'I leaned far over the bow with my ear close to the weed and heard the only sound in all the miles around – two little crabs had climbed up on a *Sargassum* sprout and were sucking audibly at the water in their gills. Then somewhere in the next valley or two a whale spouted and sank quietly.'

Beebe dived frequently and fearlessly — 'After a hundred dives or so you lose your fear' — so he was not content to wade in the shallows. He looked longingly into 'the green depths where illuminations like moonlight showed waving sea fans and milling fish far beyond the length of my hose'.

The notion of a deep-sea chamber had been discussed with President Theodore Roosevelt, a fellow naturalist/hunter, in the days when that wasn't a contradiction in terms. Roosevelt suggested a sphere, but Beebe stuck to his own idea of a cylinder. His plans were published in the *New York Times* in 1926, together with the assertion that it would not need an artificial floodlight as the depths would be 'highly illuminated by the luminescent organs of deep-sea fish', a suggestion doubted by all those who have tried to read outdoors at midnight by the glare of glow-worms. An engineer called Otis Barton wrote to him stressing that a cylinder that looked like a laundry boiler was far less resistant to pressure than a sphere. Beebe did not reply and it was several years before Barton was granted an audience.

Barton had dived with a bucket helmet as early as 1917, long before Beebe had 'dangled'. He had also fought off a shark attack. Having graduated from Columbia University as an engineer, he then studied zoology with Roy Miner at the Museum of Natural History in New York. As was then the fashion, he set out to search for dinosaurs and fossil men in Persia, but found only a tooth from an ancient uncle of the giraffe and the fez of a Sunday school teacher who had vanished four years before.

Beebe's books influenced his conversion to biology, but it was as an engineer that he was to be invaluable. Barton designed and, with his own money, built a large metal sphere with a manhole at one side and fused-quartz portholes on the opposite flank. His bathysphere (deep sphere) cost $12,000, a huge sum, and resembled 'an enormous, inflated and slightly cross-eyed bullfrog'. It was to be lowered into the sea on a hawser and had no external air supply; it was furnished with oxygen tanks and chemicals to absorb excess carbon dioxide. For the expedition to the Bahamas, Barton hired an old hulk with a winch too weak to lift the five-ton sphere, so he melted it down and cast another almost half the weight, and with walls only one and a half inches thick.

It needed twenty-eight attendants on the surface ship to tend to the sphere and its communications. The crew worked fine, but the ship, the *Ready*, was anything but. Laden with gear and three miles from shore she developed a leak. The crew, gazing over the side, saw a fish swim up to the hull and vanish inside. With none of her pumps working, she had to run for land before she sank. Thereafter a tug came out with them 'in case of need'. It would have been unfortunate if the sphere had descended only to be followed by its mother ship.

Barton dealt with the technical side of the dives, for Beebe 'had no feeling for machinery' and couldn't even drive a car. He was better at gazing at the stars through a telescope, devouring whodunits or reading Kipling out loud to the others over after-dinner whiskies and soda. Beebe also entertained the visitors that inevitably dropped in on the expeditions that were not lost in the wilds. The curator of the local museum came to call at the very time a fisherman brought in a rare species of eel in case the scientists were interested. Indeed they were, and the day ended with an undignified tug of war after which Beebe was left holding the head and the curator the tail.

Before attempting to reach depths far greater than anyone had dared before, they decided to lower the bathysphere unmanned. Imagine their dismay when, on its return to the surface, water was dripping from the closed hatch. Beebe gingerly unbolted the hatch which, with a terrifying scream, shot across the deck like a shell from a howitzer and gouged a steel winch thirty feet away. The ingress of water had squashed the air inside the sphere to the size of a tiny bubble. Once the pressure was relieved, the bubble reverted to its original size and thrust out the water at high velocity. After all the seals had been restuffed, the sphere was ready to be lowered into the ocean – with Beebe and Barton inside.

They entered through the fourteen-inch-wide hatch, crawled painfully over the steel bolts, fell inside and curled up on the cold, hard bottom of the sphere. 'I called for a cushion only to find that we had none on hand. Otis Barton climbed in after me, and we untangled our legs and got set.' Their metal cell was only four and a half feet across:

Beebe (left) & Barton cosily cooped inside the Bathysphere, after making their broadcast from the depths, 1932 (*O. Barton*)

At our signal the four-hundred-pound door was hoisted and clanged into place, sliding snugly over the ten great steel bolts. Then the huge nuts were screwed on. If either of us had time to be nervous, this would have been an excellent opportunity – carrying out Poe's idea of being sealed up, not all at once, but little by little . . . There began the most infernal racket I have ever heard. It was necessary not only to screw the nuts down hard, but to pound the wrenches with hammers to take up all possible slack. I was sure the windows would be cracked, but . . . we gradually got used to the ear-shattering reverberations. Then the utter silence settled down.

They were lowered over the side suspended on a steel hawser almost an inch thick. 'I remembered,' Beebe wrote, 'that I had read of Houdini's method of remaining in a closed coffin for a long time, and we both began conscientiously regulating our breathing and conversing in low tones.'

The initial dives did not go smoothly. At 600 feet down Beebe announced that 'only dead men have sunk deeper than this.' As if to prove him correct, water began to leak in round the hatch. Barton suggested that they abort the dive and ask to be hauled up. 'I think not,' Beebe replied. 'Don't frighten them on deck.' Meanwhile, the thick electric cable was being pushed through its seals by the pressure and was slowly coiling around Barton. 'That reminds me of the death of Laocoön in the coils of the serpent,' Beebe commented. By the time they reached the surface they had shipped over five gallons of water and Barton was ensnared by fourteen feet of serpentine cable.

On a subsequent dive, Beebe kept a record of his observations and telephone messages to the surface:

> There was the unforgettable swash and flow of bubbles and foam over the glass, and then the splendid pale brilliance of the green upper layers of the ocean . . . we were at last started on the deep, downward path . . .

> The dimming of the light was more evident between the surface and fifty feet than anywhere else, for within this zone all the warm, red rays are absorbed and the remainder of the spectrum, with its dominance of green and blue, reflected a sense of chill through our eyes long before the thermometer had dropped a degree.

> For the first 200 feet we shifted and settled, and arranged our legs and instruments for the long period of incarceration . . . We had nothing but a slow darkening to indicate that we were descending, The cable was paid out so slowly that we had no sense of movement.

> At 500 feet we had an elaborate and careful rehearsal of light signals. These were of the greatest importance, for if anything should happen to our sole line of communication – the telephone wires – a single flickering of the light would indicate at least that we were still alive . . . [On one dive

the telephone did indeed fail and their spirits plummeted, for the human voice had seemed a much surer bond with the safe world above than did the cable from which they were suspended.]

I took a careful spectroscope reading and could see about 80 per cent of purple and violet, 20 per cent, green, but no other colours. At 700 feet . . . the sun went under a blanket of cloud and before it was announced through the telephone I knew it from the intensification of the blueness . . .

When at 1,000 feet a voice reminded me that there were twenty-three hundred tons [Beebe uses the American short ton of 2,000 lbs] of water pressing in on the bathysphere, and the window against which I had my face was withstanding six and a half tons, it meant little. I watched a delicate sea creature swimming slowly along and all sense of pressure was absent . . . Here we hung for a time until my eyes could get perfectly adapted to the blue-black gloom . . . We took stock of the conditions in our little world . . . I flashed the light towards the windows and saw trickles of water coming from under the electric light screen. For a moment I had that peculiar feeling of momentary panic . . . and then I saw that all the walls showed meandering trickles of moisture, and knew it was the normal condensation on the cold steel

from the heat of our bodies. Violent fanning
every few minutes kept the air cool and fresh,
and we regulated the oxygen valve to exactly
two litres a minute. Nevertheless, it was being
used up more rapidly than we liked, so Barton
began giving his reports on the instruments in
as few words as possible and my observations
began to lack unnecessary adjectives and
adverbs . . .

Our electric light now cast a strong beam
showing as turquoise blue through the
darkness. . . . Word came down the wire that
we were being broadcast [on NBC radio and
the BBC], but a moment later this was
forgotten . . . Sealed up as we were, the human
mind utterly refused to conceive of anyone
except my assistant . . . being able to hear
what I was saying.

At 1,650 feet I recorded it as being as
black as Hades. I was running out of
reasonable similes. A school of brilliantly
illuminated lantern fish with pale green lights
swam past . . .

A little after three o'clock we reached
1,700 feet . . . beyond sunlight as far as the
human eye could tell, and from here down, for
two billion years, there had been no day or
night, no summer or winter, no passing of time
until we came to record it . . . The temperature
outside was already ten degrees lower than
that inside and the pressure had increased to

seven hundred pounds per square inch . . .

I began to ignore the passing of dozens of bright lights and . . . my eyes began to perceive outlines, to unite apparently unconnected illumination. For example, I saw seven fish which kept in sight for a time, all headed one way . . . One dashed towards me and head-on I could distinguish the flash of long fangs . . .

At 1,950 feet we got our first bad pitching. It was unexpected and I cut my lip and forehead against the window ledge and Barton struck his head against the door. This gave us the worst fright of the entire dive, and for a fraction of a minute, which seemed an exceedingly long time to us, it felt as if we had broken loose and were turning over . . . To feel the great steel ball rolling back and forth like a football, after its stolid stability on the surface, was too new a sensation to be pleasant.

At 2,200 feet, the lights were bewildering . . . I would focus on one creature and just as its outlines began to be distinct on my retina, some brilliant, animated comet or constellation would rush across the small arc of my submarine heaven and every sense would be distracted . . . I watched one gorgeous light as big as a sixpence coming steadily towards me, until, without the slightest warning, it seemed to explode, so that I jerked my head backward away from the window. What happened was

that the organism had struck against the glass
and was stimulated to a hundred brilliant
points instead of one . . .

While we hung in mid-ocean at our lowest
level of 2,200 feet, a fish poised just to the left
of my window, its elongate outline distinct . . .
wholly different from any deep-sea fish which
had yet been captured by man. It turned
slowly head-on toward me and every ray of
illumination vanished, together with its outline
and itself – it simply was not, yet I knew it had
not swung away . . .

Several minutes later, I had the most
exciting experience of the whole dive. Two
fish went very slowly by . . . at least six feet in
length. They were of the general shape of
barracudas . . . A single line of strong lights,
pale bluish, was strung down the body . . . The
undershot jaw was armed with numerous
fangs . . . There were two long tentacles
hanging down, each tipped with a pair of
separate, luminous bodies, the upper reddish,
the lower one blue. These twitched and jerked
along beneath the fish . . . I subsequently
named [it] *Bathysphaera intacta*, the
untouchable bathysphere fish . . .

But on our return to the deck . . . as I
looked out over the tossing ocean and realised
what I had been permitted to see, almost half a
mile below the surface, I knew that I should
never again look upon the stars without

> remembering their active, living counterparts
> swimming in that terrific pressure . . . many
> most delicate and fragile . . . amid this black,
> ice-cold water . . . It will remain forever the
> most vivid memory in life, solely because of
> the cosmic chill and isolation, the eternal and
> absolute darkness and the indescribable
> beauty of its inhabitants.

Later, on a three-hour dive, literally at the very end of their tether, they reached 3,028 feet, with the sphere's porthole holding back 19 tons of pressure. They had penetrated five times deeper into the ocean than anyone before them, into a place where there was only 'chill and night and death'. Beebe swore he 'would never again use the word BLACK with any conviction'. He also admitted considering 'that instant, unthinkably instant, death that would result from the least fracture of the glass or collapse of the metal. There was no possible chance of being drowned, for the first few drops would have shot through flesh and bone like steel bullets.'

Barton's worries were slightly different. He had calculated that the hawser should be able to take the strain, but had doubts that the ship's winch could haul up over a ton of sphere together with two tons of hawser. The steam boilers powering the winch were working well above their rated pressure and the effort was audible. If the winch and its donkey engine were pulled out of gear with each other, the cable would unwind at a terrifying speed and the sphere would plummet into the abyss. Fortunately, it never happened.

In a darkness twinkling with luminescent creatures, Beebe observed several species new to science, but the creatures of the deep were so fantastic that many of his discoveries were discounted at the time. During the Second World War, the sphere was drafted and sent on a secret mission to study the effects of depth charges for the US navy. It retired to the American Museum of Natural History to perch alongside Miner's coral reef.

Barton went on to make underwater films and, in 1949, without Beebe and in an improved sphere, his 'eyeball on a string' penetrated to a depth of 4,500 feet.

Some years before, Beebe had married Elswyth Thane, a writer half his age who had based the hero of her first novel on him. Together they now refurbished a run-down farm in Vermont, and she wrote another novel, *Reluctant Farmer*, in which a young writer sets up home with an elderly naturalist. Beebe found the New England winters, and perhaps also the marriage, too cold, and bought a place in Bermuda where he spent six months each year. In 1949 he acquired land in Trinidad and set up a tropical research laboratory. He donated it to the New York Zoological Society, but stayed on as the director and worked there until shortly before his death.

He was depressed to learn that one of his jungle study sites had been replaced with banana plantations, that the seal colonies he had studied in Guadeloupe had been slaughtered for dog food and the endemic iguanas he had written about in the Galápagos Islands had been exterminated by bored American soldiers using them for target practice. His energies were turned to preventing the depredation to reefs caused by tourists and divers. All the destructive collecting of his youth was forgotten and biographies would claim that one of his major contributions to science lay in his abiding concern with conservation.

His health declined and a minor stroke slurred his speech, although he remained 'playful' to the last. One night he regaled a visitor with gory stories of the dining habits of the local vampire bats, then sneaked into the guest's bedroom at midnight to tweak his toe and awaken him with a scream.

Beebe had hoped to expire of heart failure upon witnessing some new, heart-stopping wonder, but he died in bed of the 'old man's friend', pneumonia. He was buried in the cemetery in Port of Spain.

In spite of his weighty monographs on birds and fish, dozens of scientific articles and the many new species he named (some, to the dismay of other taxonomists, based on specimens seen only fleetingly looming out of the darkness towards the window of the bathysphere), he is remembered not as a scientist but as a popu-lariser. Experimentation was foreign to him. He was largely a high-powered bird-watcher and fish-finder, but he was also a stargazer. There are few underwater explorers that were not inspired by his books. Rachel Carson wrote in her bestseller, *The Sea Around Us* that her absorption in the mystery and meaning of the sea had been stimulated by the friendship and encouragement of William Beebe.

Under water, he claimed, it was as if he were a 'half-blind old man, crippled with rheumatism and palsy and dropped . . . into the busiest of city streets and requested to narrate the happenings about him, and give to them some sort of explanation.' Yet few have bettered his descriptions of the magic of being beneath the sea:

> I submerged near the foot of the great cliffs,
> and . . . disciplined myself into a greater
> realisation of the wonder of it. I think my first

surprise was of the constant movement of
everything, not so much individually as of the
whole in relation to the rocks and bottom. I
knew of course that the boat was rising and
falling with every surge, which heaved and
settled in turn as each wave passed to break
against the cliffs. I found this same motion
extended downward, with less force, until at
thirty feet it all but died away. At present in
about twenty feet of water I felt it strongly. I
would be sitting quietly without the slightest
tremor, when, gently and without shock, every
fish in sight, every bit of weed or hydroid, the
anchor rope, the shadow of the boat, the hose
and myself swayed toward the land. One
could resist by clinging firmly to the rock, but
the supreme joy, because of its impossibility in
the air above, was to balance carefully and let
oneself be wafted through space and deposited
safely on the next rock. There followed a
period of complete rest, and back again
everything would come. It was so soothing, so
rhythmical, that one yielded to it at times in a
daze of sheer enjoyment.

His books assembled armies of adjectives to paint the underwater landscape. He was the first to describe sea lions and pen-
guins swimming under water, and diving cormorants pursuing sea
bass beneath the waves. This 'wonderer beneath the sea' never lost
his love for that place of 'astonishing happenings, of exquisite
magic, of ineffable, colourful mystery'. Is it surprising that he

sometimes found the world overhead drab and uneventful by comparison?

Beebe became famous. In addition to his books and the broadcast from the deep, there were cartoons in the *New Yorker*. H. G. Wells' short story, *In the Abyss*, and Dennis Wheatley's best-seller, *They Found Atlantis*, were both based on descents in a bathysphere. Not content with the real wonders that Beebe described, both sets of fictitious explorers found humanoids in the deep. Our vanity dictates that only creatures like ourselves are interesting.

Although few readers would have followed Beebe's entreaty not to 'die without having borrowed, stolen, purchased or made a helmet of sorts, to glimpse for yourself this new world', he had awakened the general public to the excitement of exploring the depths of the ocean.

Other scientists would don 'milk churn' helmets to study the sea, and the most important of these was an Englishman called Jack Kitching.

Little devil fish first described by Beebe (*W. Beebe*)

Jack Kitching about to ramble over underwater valleys, Carsaig, Scotland, 1937. In the background is his wife-to-be, Evelyn

(*Photograph by Professor Russell Lumsden*)

Running
on treacle

John Alwyne Kitching 1908–1996

When he was six years old, Jack Kitching was taken on holiday to Cornwall. Holding his father's hand, he gazed into the tide pools and roamed the fields searching for grasshoppers and butterflies. Later that same week his father failed to return from a walk. He had collapsed from a heart attack and never recovered. That first fateful holiday had forged Jack's life; he had lost his father and found an enduring love of nature that would eventually lead him beneath the waves.

It was July 1931 at Wembury Bay on the Devon coast. The diver was dressed in a rugby shirt and shorts but as summer set in with its usual severity, he donned a woollen jumper, tweed trousers and stout walking shoes. It was as if he were going for a ramble over rock-strewn valleys, which I suppose he was.

On his head was a milk churn with a window inserted at the front, and 150 feet of garden hose attached to replenish the air. The lead weights that kept the helmet in place were so heavy that they could not be attached until the diver was submerged.

The diver was Jack Kitching, now 23 years old and a zoologist newly graduated from Cambridge. As soon as he had

Descending into a submarine gulley in 1933
(*By permission of Rosemary Anderson*)

completed the study of this submerged gully in Devon he would
be off to Argyll in Scotland to plunge into the Sound of Jura,
diving there every summer for the next five years. Without a
diving suit, it was difficult to withstand the cold for more than
twenty minutes at a time, but, by working in shifts, he and his colleagues managed to put in an hour a day under water. Frequent
diving led to a 'greatly increased appetite for sugar and treacle', a
proclivity he retained for the rest of his life, whether diving or not.
He had singular dietary requirements. When refuelling for the
next task he often chose peanut butter and jam or golden syrup
on sausages and bacon, claiming that 200 million Americans can't
be wrong. On one occasion he covered a slice of currant bread
with peanut butter, syrup, raspberry jam and Bengal hot chutney,
describing the flavour as 'interesting'. He even consumed a bar of

chocolate writhing with maggots. 'Not bad,' he decided. 'Full of protein.'

His diving helmet had an internal telephone, the microphone almost completely filled with wax and encased in a toy balloon to keep it dry. The intention was to dictate notes to the surface where they would be written down prior to publication, but the message he most frequently transmitted was: 'More air! More air!'

On the surface his fiancée, Evelyn, held the safety line whilst another helper laboured over two foot-pumps designed to inflate tyres, and prayed for the moment they would swap jobs. Years later one of the pumpers admitted: 'Sometimes we'd make Jack suffer a bit by easing back on the air.'

Armed only with hedging shears to cut his way through the dense kelp, Jack, like a ghostly gardener, trudged down to a depth of 40 feet through the forest into the 'park' of more widely spaced plants below. From here 'it was possible through the misty water to see the park extending downwards much further on the steeply sloping bottom.' He was the first biologist to see the kelp forest under water.

But Kitching was no underwater tourist; he was determined to do some science under the sea. He provided the first detailed description of the forest and the plants and animals that lived on the kelp and beneath its shade. He censused every snail and seaweed and explained their distribution with respect to substratum, slope, situation and light. Using photocells and a series of filters, he recorded the amount and quality of light at different depths and beneath the canopy. It was as dense as any tropical forest and acted as a breakwater as well as a parasol. Removing some of the kelp showed that the forest could regenerate and restore the canopy within a year. It was an astonishing piece of work for its time.

He was appointed lecturer in experimental zoology at Bristol University in 1937 and the students there changed the direction of his life's work. They had just enjoyed a field trip to Lough Ine, a beautiful marine 'lake' in southern Ireland, and asked Jack to organise a proper scientific expedition for the following year. One of the students was John Ebling, and thus began a partnership that would last for 39 years.

Jack's Quaker upbringing had failed to give him either God or the Quaker dislike of ritual. At Lough Ine everything was ritualised: the coffee-making ceremony, the washing-up performance, even the Sunday sing-song came to mimic a Sunday service – a biscuit, sherry, a song book of ancient tunes.

The war intervened and Jack was drafted to the University of Toronto to join a group of physiologists working in collaboration with the Royal Canadian Air Force, the USAF and the RAF on problems of pressing military importance. They came up with electrically heated boots and mittens to stop the pilot freezing to the controls at altitude, and water-filled flying suits to prevent him blacking out when pulling out of a dive. During such a manoeuvre the water rushed down to the pilot's legs and by compressing them kept the blood in his brain.

Jack's speciality was trying to ensure the survival of pilots that had ditched in the sea. He wrote a report entitled 'The measurement of internal body temperature of men exposed to severe cold'. One of the men exposed was, of course, Jack. He helped to devise a survival suit which resembled a blimp from which all the air had escaped, and then asked to be dumped in the Atlantic off Nova Scotia in winter 'to see how I get on'. The 'Aids' kit contained fishing gear and a repair outfit so there were plenty of hooks and needles around to puncture his rubber dinghy. He was also given matches should he need to light a fire. His survival rations included pea soup powder which was 'unappetising' and chocolate that was 'nauseating' – severe criticism from a man usually fearless in the face of food.

He survived, and three months after the trial, the survival suit was in production and being issued to bomber crews. In 1947 Jack was awarded the OBE – 'For Ordinary Bloody Effort,' he boasted.

From 1946 onwards Jack led annual expeditions to study the ecology of Lough Ine. He took up diving again in 1948 to study the rapids through which the sea rushed into and out of the Lough so fiercely that diving was only possible for fifteen minutes either side of slack water. By now he had a proper diver's dry-suit and huge lead-soled boots, but still had a milk churn on his head.

At first the team studied the distribution of animals and

Kitching with sickle & seaweed emerging from Lough Ine Rapids, 1951
(*Photograph by Professor Michael Sleigh*)

plants in relation to waves and current. Jack worked under water
harvesting seaweeds with an enormous sickle and hauling dozens
of boulders to the surface to examine their fauna. He designed an
ingenious miniature diving bell for the boulders so that they
could be enclosed under water whilst all the water was gently
pumped out, leaving the silt on their surface undisturbed to be
examined when a boulder still in its bell was lifted out of the
water. Almost every day for a month he hauled up rocks. A colleague described this in a doggerel diary reminiscent of the verse
in *Rupert* books:

> Jack, in his frog suit, wades about
> And tries to lift the blighters out.
> Sometimes they come, sometimes they stay,
> For him to try another day.

If the diving was energetic work, pumping air down to the diver
was a sentence with hard labour. The pumpers cheered when the
machine broke down.

> No diving could take place. With luck,
> The gadget's permanently stuck.

As more and more boulders were collected, the team wearied and
the verse became terser:

> July 8th –   To get some further information,
>   We did another boulder station.

> July 9th –   In the morning, once again,
>   We boulder by the quay and then . . .

July 13th – Today we really thought we ought
               To gather boulders at site nought.

July 18th – Jack's diving suit has sprung a leak.
               He found it out in Eddy Creek.

July 19th – The suit's repaired and we must do
               A good day's work – and Tuesday's too!

July 21st – The daily round, the common task.
               What did we do? Well need you ask?

Kitching getting all dressed up with somewhere to go, Lough Ine, early 1950s
(*Photograph by Ronald Bassindale, with permission of Pam Bassindale*)

Nor was it all fun for the diver. By the early 1950s Jack had replaced his helmet with a full face mask. It was still supplied with air from a pump on the surface but now he couldn't bail out if it filled with water. During one emergency, two students hauled his head above the surface whilst others pumped like mad to keep the sea water at bay. Jack swore through the intercom and made intermittent gurgling noises as the water submerged his mouth and nose. On another occasion his false teeth escaped and had to be retrieved from the sea floor.

Kitching had loved the sea since his youth when he was a keen yachtsman. He had studied classics at school, for in those days only weak pupils did mathematics and science. He opted for biology at Cambridge, but marine biology was not initially his main line of research. He was probably the most distinguished experimental zoologist to study the protozoa, those tiny aquatic animalcules that swim in an almost invisible world. Kitching revealed how such vulnerable single-celled organisms adjusted their water balance and coped with the stresses of daily life.

He also found that microscopic animals were useful for studying how cell processes are affected by high pressures such as those endured in the ocean deeps. In laboratory experiments the organisms often became befuddled and forgot how to grow or reproduce or to get into reverse. In recognition of his research he was elected a Fellow of the Royal Society in 1960. In 1964 he enjoyed being a founding professor at the new University of East Anglia, designing the Biology curriculum and even the laboratories.

I first met Jack in 1964 at Lough Ine. On entering his laboratory, I was stunned to see the legs of a corpse dangling through the loft opening. 'My diving suit,' he explained. 'It keeps intruders away.'

He was tall with long lean legs and his nose was exfoliating from too much sun. If he had been a chicken you wouldn't have eaten him. 'Call me Jack,' he said in a voice like a distant foghorn softened by mist.

He wore tatty shorts and a sweater with large pieces missing. This was his typical field attire, grade three. He had five grades of clothes, differentiated by how much fabric remained. Grade five's were just a cobweb of threads. If it was cold, he would simply continue to don sweaters until most of the holes were occluded. Once, at home, his wife decided he needed a new sports jacket and escorted him to the shops. He was none too pleased to be dragged away from his beloved garden. Nor was she overjoyed when, in a high-class men's outfitters in Norwich, he removed his coat to reveal a grade-four jumper.

He brought to Lough Ine only the minimum of personal effects, as befits an expedition. He left his gear behind at base camp each year, including traditional pyjamas striped like an antique deckchair and with the flies torn right around to the back seam so that the legs would have departed in different directions had they not been tethered together by the cord.

Jack's Quaker upbringing perhaps contributed to his stiffness in company. Laughing didn't come naturally to him; it was as if he had learned it from a book. For politeness, he uttered a restrained guffaw that really did sound like 'Ha! Ha! Ha!' But very occasionally, if you could take him by surprise with something that really amused him, he would forget his laughing lessons and, without making a sound, tilt his head backwards until tears streamed down his face.

We spent one soft Irish summer measuring the amount of light reaching the seaweed at different depths. The kelp forest cut out over 90 per cent of it and beneath the canopy there was perpetual twilight. Beautiful, light-hungry carmine seaweeds perched on the top of the kelp stalks to grab better illumination, but those on the rock below made do with the brief but brilliant sun flecks that flashed down when the canopy parted.

Jack sent me down to retrieve the light-measuring photocells and, whilst waiting in the boat for me to return, he was accosted by a local, curious as to why someone without a rod or pots should be bobbing about on the ocean.

'Is it fishing you are?' he asked.

'No,' replied Jack at his most precisely obtuse. 'We are monitoring irradiance amidst *Laminaria* in the sublittoral zone.'

'Ah yes, I was thinking that's what it would be.' But he circled around close by to see what was *really* going on.

I surfaced and handed Jack the photocell. In a loud voice he said, 'Is the warhead intact, Carruthers?'

Whilst I pondered what he was talking about, I noticed a chap rowing hell for leather to the shore. Next day there wasn't a person in town that hadn't heard of the misguided missile that had plunged into the sea off Lough Ine and made the whole place radioactive.

Just outside the lough a cave bores 100 metres into the rock, straight as an engineer's tunnel. The zonation of seaweeds as you penetrate horizontally into the cave is almost identical to that found by a diver outside as he descends. Yet the conditions are different. As you go deeper, the light gets dimmer, but it also changes colour, for water absorbs light selectively. In the cave there was the same dimming of the light but without these changes in its quality. We were conducting a natural experiment to see which properties of light most influenced the plants, so we set up photocells to measure light of different wavelengths at various distances inside the cave. When the work was finished, the photocells had to be recovered. Jack had planned to do it the next day, but the weather began to deteriorate.

'The wind is getting up in the west,' said Jack.

'So it is,' I replied.

'It looks as if it will get much worse before morning. I'm concerned for the photocells in the cave.'

'Do you want to go get them?'

'I think we should.'

So we slipped down the Rapids in the watery moonlight and it was almost midnight when we entered the cave. We eased into the flawless dark, but as we pulled up the light cells their tethering ropes lit up like iridescent green worms. A great gob of phosphorescence glowed on the blade of the oar, but a torch revealed nothing.

One of the lines was adrift.

'It has come loose,' said Jack dejectedly.

'So it has,' I agreed.

'It's way out of reach. We may lose it in the storm.'

'Would you like me to dive down and get it?'

'Without your gear? Would you?'

I stripped naked and slipped over the side into the chill water and retrieved the apparatus. Under water the outline of my body was etched in green sparks.

'Trevor recovered the missing photocell,' Jack wrote years later, 'and came up glowing from head to foot in brilliant phosphorescence – very appropriate.'

What he said at the time was, 'If only I had a scalpel, I could scrape off a sample.'

Jack was an outdoor man who would readily wade into the frigid sea for samples, but I never saw him submerge for pleasure. I will never forget the rattling rhythm of his rowing, topocher ker plunk, topocher ker plunk, or the clatter of him jogging through the laboratory shouting, 'Busy, busy' when you tried to attract his attention.

He loved walking, but never a casual stroll, only a brisk march to waft away the cobwebs. Trailing a string of students, he would stride overland through bayoneted brambles, stinging nettles and head-high bracken laden with ticks. Twenty ticks later he would sit for a while and offer round a bent warm bar of Bournville chocolate from his back pocket.

Jack, the clockwork man, always led the way because he had the longest stride and was oblivious to pubs. He intended to progress at the double by the shortest route and was irritated if the road wound without reason. When in his seventies and after a whole day of trudging cross-country, he was once offered a lift, but refused. 'No thank you,' he said indignantly. 'I need the exercise.'

Jack had only two speeds – on and off. Perhaps because he was so active he was inclined to fall asleep at any time. Having slept well, and often, he gained perverse pleasure from waking the sluggish students at dawn. Once he shook me and shouted, 'Quickly, hold this!' I shot bolt upright in bed, then began to slump forward like a dog nodding before the fire. As I rallied, I realised I was white-knuckled from gripping a rope. I forced myself awake and emerged from the tent to see the rope trailing away down the site. Bare-footed and in my pyjamas I staggered through the dew-drenched grass down to the quay. The rope was attached to a boat floating out in the Lough. He also tried a variant of this, giving each end of the line to students in different tents and telling both of them to pull.

He preferred the noisy methods of arousal. Once he in-flated and tied a plastic bag to make a balloon and then jumped on it to make it bang, but in his enthusiasm he leapt too high and knocked himself out on a low beam. His favourite was the 'Irish warthog'. He would pour a little water into a plastic bottle which he then inserted beneath the tent flap. When squeezed rhythmically it belched loudly. If that didn't work, he flattened cans with a spade.

One year we were having trouble with rats around the camp and I suppose they must have been on my mind when I went to sleep. Next morning Jack devised a novel alarm call. He fixed a large tin funnel to a length of hosepipe. The plan was to slip the improvised trumpet under the skirt of my tent, push it towards my ear and blow a loud reveille. It was 6.0 a.m. when I began to surface. Something was scratching at the wall of the tent, trying to get in. Rats! Only half awake, I grabbed the nearest weapon – a large wooden mallet for whacking in tent pegs – and launched a frenzied attack on the unseen enemy, blow after blow, until I heard a groan. Rats squeak, I reasoned. It was a very deep squeak.

Jack lay on the ground, stunned, clutching his head and a sad, flattened funnel. He never again used that particular method for rousing me.

Back at the University of East Anglia, his pleasures were having all the laboratory windows open to let the winter in, or blasting them out when his experiments on the effects of pressure went wrong or, best of all, overtaking much younger colleagues on the stairs.

He could be awkward, and in meetings he was often reasonable to the point of unreasonableness. Colleagues despaired and rarely mentioned his name without adding, 'a difficult man'.

I knew him only at Lough Ine – Jack gone feral – but always suspected that he of the cloven pyjamas and grade-five sweaters was the real Jack. Lough Ine was a time to play Swallows and Amazons, and to do good field research.

Kitching and his collaborators revolutionised marine biology by showing that it was possible to carry out ecological experiments in the sea rather than the laboratory. They pioneered experiments in which organisms were transplanted from one site to another to see how they got on, or key predators were added or removed and the repercussions monitored. Such experiments transformed our way of studying sea-floor communities and marine ecologists worldwide have adopted their approach. Paul Dayton, a distinguished American ecologist, once told me he had visited Ireland on a pilgrimage to Kitching's laboratory. 'For an old atheist like me,' he wrote, 'it was about as close to religion as I could get.'

Kitching kept on researching at Lough Ine every summer until long after he had retired. At Lough Ine he greeted the first-year undergraduates with 'Call me Jack,' and amazed them with his energy and enthusiasm for the work, his willingness to muck in with the most menial tasks, and an ability to eat anything whether it was edible or not.

But like William Beebe before him, a series of strokes slowed him down. His voice faded to a whisper, and so did his writing. It had always been small but now it was minute, the tracks left by a tiny lost spider, trailing down to fall off the page.

In 1993 he entered a nursing home. Jack, who once bestrode the hills, could no longer walk nor stand. He who had kept peanut butter factories in full production could no longer feed himself. He did not take kindly to being dependent on others.

Then he sank into silence. Only one bright moment remained. He received a copy of the marine biology textbook he had started and a colleague had finished. He spent many hours looking at it, slowly turning the pages as if they were the pages of his life. He died in bed at the age of eighty-seven.

Jack's first publication involving diving work appeared in 1934, his last in 1990, and the research continues through the many marine ecologists he encouraged and inspired. Lough Ine, now, thanks to him, a statutory marine reserve, has become a Mecca for diving biologists. There can be few diving experiences to match lying beneath the kelp forest in the Rapids as the flow accelerates, and watching the great plants writhing and thrashing above your head, until, that is, the current whips off your mask, steals your fins and spits you out into the Lough.

Bullock Island cave

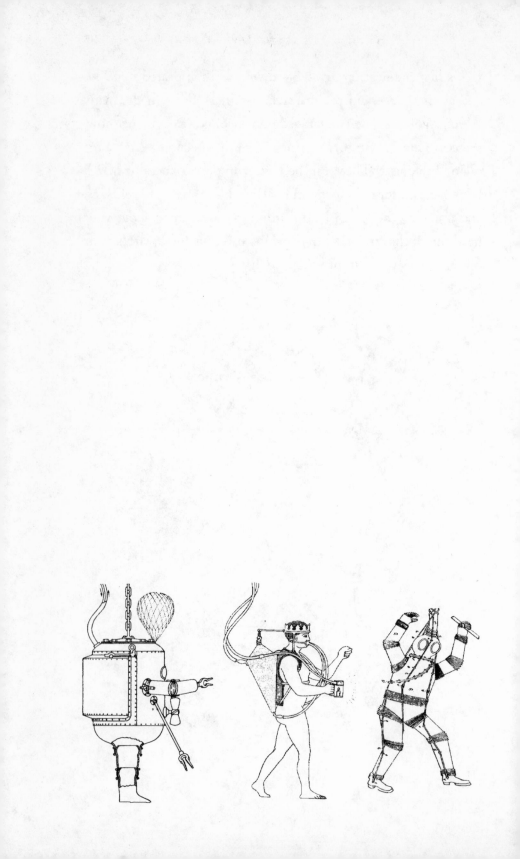

THINKERS AND
SINKERS

Scientists were fascinated by the problems of surviving at depths where oxygen is poisonous and the weight of the water above could crush an elephant. Today oceanographers, for a joke, attach a large polystyrene cup to equipment lowered into the depths. It returns with the air squeezed out, and the size of a thimble.

The diver has lungs and sinuses full of air, and the ears are vulnerable, for only a thin membrane separates the water outside from the air within. In the mid-eighteenth century, pearl divers in the Caribbean were not thought to have come of age until they had returned to the surface with 'blood gushing from their eyes, mouth and nose', and the more daring had been known to drop dead from 'congestion and haemorrhaging'. Even William Beebe believed that there would be no return for the diver from 40 metres, for 'he would be unable to rise again'.

Terrible though pressure is in reality, it held even deeper fears in the mind. It was believed that it would crush the incompressible water itself, increasing its viscosity, so that any object that sank would not reach the bottom, only descend to the depth at which it encountered water of the same density as itself. Thus wooden ships and their cannons would come to settle at different depths. Worst of all, bodies committed to the deep would hang for ever at their proscribed depth in a suspended graveyard.

Doubts were expressed about whether submarine telephone cables could possibly reach the bottom and, if they did, would the voices traversing the ocean be squashed to 'a mouse's squeaking'?

Yet plummeting to the depths is far less dangerous than returning towards the 'safety' of the surface when your lungs could explode and your blood froth like soda water. Divers were being maimed and killed and the pressure was on to find the cause.

Beebe and Barton's sphere being menaced by the untouchable bathysphere fish (*By permission of Random House UK Ltd*)

John Haldane in a coal mine, wearing his prototype breathing apparatus
(*By permission of Professor J. M. Mitchison*)

The absent-
minded professor

John Scott Haldane 1860–1936

Physiologists who were rarely tempted to dive could, nonetheless, be fascinated by the consequences of working and surviving under water. The most important of these was John Scott Haldane.

He arose from sturdy Scottish stock; they were one of only fifteen families in Britain who could name every ancestor through the male line from AD 1250, the chief advantage of which was 'protection against respect for the voice of the Establishment'. Haldanes had been Lords of Gleneagles since the thirteenth century. One had married Montrose's sister, another had fallen at Flodden. John's brother, Richard, Lord Haldane of Cloan, became Lord Chancellor in Asquith's cabinet. Haldanes were achievers and every New Year's Eve the matriarch would gather the family around her bed and they would have to recite their accomplishments during the past year and expectations for the year ahead.

John graduated in medicine from Edinburgh University and practised briefly at the Royal Infirmary until he was appointed demonstrator at the University College of Dundee. He retained an interest in medicine and after rats carrying plague were reported from the Central Hotel in Glasgow, he always stayed there in the hope of seeing an infected rodent expire in his room. The main benefit of his medical days was, however, a suitcase bearing the words, LONDON FEVER HOSPITAL, which for years he carried with him on train journeys to ensure that mothers whisked away their rowdy children and left him alone in the compartment.

His main research interest was in the influence of air quality on human health, a subject that would fascinate him for the rest of his life. He analysed the air in slum housing, factories, schools, and sewers ripe with the whiff of bitter oranges or raw jute, depending on which factory was disgorging. He demolished the then widely held view that typhoid was caused by a 'miasma' that was inhaled from the drains. He had shown, as he put it, that 'germs don't jump'.

In the Dundee slums, where there were sometimes six or even eight to a bed, if there was a bed at all, he found that overnight levels of carbon dioxide and bacteria rose alarmingly. For the undernourished inhabitants the slums were incubators for disease. If his experiences there did not make him a radical, they certainly kept him one.

Later he would stalk the London Underground collecting the smoky air in a jar held out of the train window and sucking up samples with a tube. The levels of deadly carbon monoxide were so high that his findings led to the electrification of the lines. He was also appointed as a Gas Referee for London and then the whole of England to check the quality of domestic coal gas, a substance he 'held in low esteem'. However, the pay for this part-time post almost doubled his university salary.

In 1887 he married Kathleen Trotter, of a wealthy Scottish family. They spent their honeymoon locked in the bedroom with her taking dictation of a draft of his new book on vitalism (the belief that the workings of life cannot be understood solely in mechanistic terms). Her new home was littered with unpaid bills and unfinished manuscripts and she soon realised that this would not be an ordinary marriage. She lamented that Haldane had cupboards full of clothes 'which, when the drawers were opened . . . flew out to meet me. I have never seen such a flight of moths.'

In the year of their marriage he took up a temporary appointment as a teaching assistant in his uncle's department of Physiology at Oxford University. The professor's wife asked all the 'right people' to call on Kathleen, but a servant hid their calling cards because she considered that Mrs H. 'had far more visitors than was good for her'.

Haldane, the proud father, giving his two-year-old son, Jack, a ride on his bike (*By permission of Professor J. M. Mitchison*)

Soon there was a son, Jack, and five years later a daughter, Naomi (later Naomi Mitchison, the writer). John agreed not to discuss physiology 'below the diaphragm' at the dining table, nor air his atheist and liberal ideas in front of the children. He allowed Kathleen to imbue them with religion (the Bible with 'the dirty bits left out') and her notions of nation and empire and patrio-tism. This resulted in both the children winning prizes for scrip-ture, but Naomi became a socialist councillor and Jack a communist.

When elected a Fellow of the Royal Society in 1897 he was still only a lowly demonstrator at the university. Not long after this his uncle transferred to the Chair of Medicine and John was bitterly disappointed not to step into the vacant Chair of Physiology. His uncle, wary of accusations of nepotism, did not support him, so John accepted a college fellowship instead. He loved life at New College, Oxford, especially the formal dinners with their rituals.

He had now become fascinated by gases in mines. Under-ground explosions were commonplace and after every disaster Haldane snatched up his mining helmet and rushed off to inves-tigate. To reassure his wife he was safe, he sent telegrams that were so incoherent they merely confirmed that he was suffering from exposure to one poisonous gas or another. Sometimes the same telegram arrived several times, when he was so befuddled that he had forgotten the previous one. Whilst he was away, the children pored over the lurid engravings in such books of father's as *Mining Disasters* and *Dangerous Trades*.

Haldane found that most of the fatalities in mine explosions resulted not from the blast, but from suffocation by exposure to carbon monoxide or even pure nitrogen, or from the delayed trauma of extensive but superficial skin burns. He proposed measures to combat each of these, and was the first to show con-clusively that pneumoconiosis resulted from the inhalation of dust. He conducted experiments in his laboratory even though the Home Office refused to license it. He wrote to them declaring that he would do the experiments anyway and, if they jailed him, every miner in Britain would come out on strike. The licence was granted.

To test the effects of carbon monoxide poisoning he inhaled it whilst recording his symptoms and taking samples of his own blood to analyse the amount in his haemoglobin. When it reached 56 per cent saturation he could neither walk nor stand. Samples of blood taken from some asphyxiated miners had levels only 4 per cent higher.

Haldane became the director of the colliery owners' research laboratory at Doncaster and, known to half the miners in Yorkshire as 'the Doctor', was frequently seen under ground sampling the air or measuring the thickness of dust. He took down his son, Jack, for the first time when he was only four and 'very frightened'. A few years later they got lost in a maze of galleries, a miner eerily singing somewhere in the dark distance. They crawled into a shaft contaminated with methane and he told Jack to stand up and recite the 'Friends, Romans, countrymen' speech. Within a few moments he passed out and collapsed into the breathable air below. Thus Jack learned that 'fire damp' was lighter than air and was not lethal – at least in the short term.

To demonstrate that coal dust was responsible for most underground explosions, an experimental 'gallery' 100 feet long was fabricated on the surface from large old boilers welded end to end. The ledges inside were powdered with coal dust and a small charge was detonated at one end. The explosion shot along the pipe and tore the last two boilers to bits. Haldane and his son stood over 300 yards away, but a huge portion flew over their heads. Later experiments showed that limestone dust could inhibit the explosions.

Family holidays were taken in Cornwall so that father could study hookworm in tin miners. He took Jack down a shaft on the great 'man engine', a forty-five-minute descent into the abyss, stepping from one reciprocating ladder to the other in the darkness.

Haldane's understanding of the importance of carbon monoxide poisoning was applied to make mining safer. His experiments led to the introduction of mice and then canaries into mines as an early-warning system. Tests of mine rescue equipment showed that much of it was useless, so he devised better. Practical problems such as these were the stimulus for much of his physiological work and the results greatly reduced the risks in several hazardous professions. For him the application of new knowledge to the welfare of mankind was the greatest objective of science. He sacrificed much valuable research time to sit on government enquiries and Royal Commissions and in berating the Home Office when they were slow to improve industrial safety.

Delegations of mine managers were entertained at the Haldanes' home and treated well, although Kathleen was 'not too partial to the working classes'. She was shocked when the offspring of prosperous tradesmen began to appear at her children's private school. 'Of course, no dentist was a gentleman and one could never meet socially.' Even the wives of the heads of university colleges were often, according to her daughter, 'far from being the people my mother would have considered her social equals'. It is difficult to imagine the horror she must have felt that her husband spent his working days with miners, sewage workers and railwaymen. She had banned *The Railway Children* from the nursery because the young heroine kisses a porter.

Fame was no excuse for 'letting the side down'. Marie Stopes was welcome when she was an expert on fossil plants and used to drop in to 'discuss the coal measures'. Then she published *Married Love* . . .

When young Jack published a book on the future of science which prophesied test-tube babies, Oxford talked of nothing else and his father was embarrassed by the jibes. Mrs Haldane wrote to Julian Huxley to express her concerns for 'the senior partner': 'Will you abstain altogether from poking fun at him on account of it? . . . I had no idea until today how really unhappy he is – odd people these Liberals and no accounting for them! . . . Keep people off him, or he'll hate you all! (which is not only sad for him but extremely inconvenient for me).'

Haldane remained on good terms with his brother Richard, Viscount Haldane. Richard had served on the Explosives Committee at the War Office and offered to give a talk which John advertised as 'A public lecture on explosives by Mr R. B. Haldane MP, illustrated by experiments conducted by Professor J. S. Haldane'. The police saw the poster and arrived early to clear the front three rows before the professor's explosions cleared them more dramatically.

The brothers also collaborated on a book on philosophy and in 1890 went off to Germany together to consult leading philosophers. There was another more important trip in 1912. Richard was now Secretary of State for War and the government were concerned over the Germans' accelerating programme for building warships. They were anxious to avoid an expensive and dangerous arms-race. Perhaps informal talks would be better than a confrontational government mission. Richard was also Vice-Chancellor of Bristol University and under this guise he could visit Berlin to study their system of technical education. Brother John, a physiologist, would accompany him to complete the smoke screen. It fooled no one. German reporters besieged their hotel and John fielded their questions. The reporters decided that he was Prime Minister Asquith in disguise and there to make a treaty. They did indeed negotiate a paper agreement after a parley with German ministers and Admiral Tirpitz. Thirty years later son Jack would be instrumental in the sinking of the pride of the German fleet – the battleship *Tirpitz*.

Both John and Richard received honorary degrees from Birmingham University. They travelled up on the train together, heavily guarded by Scotland Yard detectives to protect them from suffragettes.

John and Kathleen lived in the same house in Oxford for over sixty years (it would later become Wolfson College). Although it was dark and cluttered, the wallpaper was by William Morris and the bathroom had de Morgan tiles. The number of servants grew to a include a butler and housemaids, a nurse, a coachman for the landau and later an alcoholic chauffeur for the Daimler.

Beyond his study in the attic, John Haldane had kitted out a laboratory with an air-tight chamber so that he could investigate the effects of various gases on the experimenters within. He sometimes enlisted Naomi to keep an eye on the researcher and, if he collapsed, to drag him out of the chamber and perform artificial respiration. Best of all, she and Jack loved to sneak into the empty laboratory to chase globules of escaped mercury across the floor, make funny voices by sniffing nitrogen, or get giddy on chloroform.

Haldane could now work almost entirely at home. He invariably took milk and plum cake for midnight supper, then worked throughout the night and rose in time to have lunch for breakfast. He usually had several different lines of research in hand, keeping track of very diverse lines of enquiry. This degree of organisation and acuity did not permeate his private life. For years he operated with a watch that had lost its minute hand and had to estimate smaller fractions of time from the hour hand alone. As he never set the watch he also had to add a correction for its increasing inaccuracy – yet he never missed a train. He also had a deep suspicion of new-fangled devices such as typewriters and slide rules and from a very early age son Jack performed many of his calculations.

When Kathleen was confined to bed with measles a mouse ran across her face. A mousetrap caught it the next day, much to John's dismay. 'You killed my mouse?' he asked disbelievingly, making her feel like a murderer. Although he used mice, he disapproved of experiments on animals and 'never used an animal if a man would do'. He trained himself to ignore fear and 'preferred to experiment on himself or other human beings who were sufficiently interested in the work to ignore pain, much as a soldier would 'risk his life or endure wounds in order to gain victory'. The family motto was, after all, 'Suffer'. When young Naomi fell heavily and cried, her father made it clear that this was 'strictly forbidden in the code of courage'. He was not innately brave; he had no head for heights and was too nervous to learn to swim, but once he was engrossed in a project, he was fearless. His example was to greatly influence young Jack, who would later also conduct dangerous experiments, with himself and his colleagues as guinea-pigs.

According to his wife, the carpet in Haldane's study was 'hidden under layers of paper, the desk piled high . . . chairs laden with reports and notes and sheets of calculations'. When, in spring-cleaning mode, she asked if the carpet could be lifted and beaten, he readily agreed, 'as long as you don't move any of the papers'.

In the laboratory, where he loved messing about with rubber tubing and mercury, he expected the experimental procedures to be meticulous. But lurking in a drawer where odds and ends of apparatus were kept was an old stick of dynamite growing brittle with age.

Aldous Huxley lived with the Haldanes when he came up to Oxford in 1915. His pale face and stook of hair were perched unsteadily on an etiolated body and he was so long-limbed that no furniture could contain him; his arms dangled over the backs of sofas and his stork's legs folded around chairs. Already half-blind, he had an attractive, vulnerable look. He acted in Naomi's first plays. She wished he would kiss her, but he never did.

Huxley wrote of the most appalling tea party 'with a Belgian professor speaking in German with Haldane, his wife chatting to Jack in French', leaving poor Aldous 'in no-man's land . . . hurling words of English . . . The resulting strain was fearful.'

Being a family friend didn't inhibit Aldous from including Haldane in his novel, *Point Counter Point*, as Edward Tantamount, a scientist out of kilter with the clock and up to esoteric antics in his attic laboratory. Tantamount, 'who was in all but intellect a kind of child', worked on the regeneration of the lost parts of newts. 'Newts?' asks an acquaintance. 'Those things that swim? . . . But how do they lose their parts?' 'Well, in the laboratory,' Tantamount explains, 'they lose them because we cut them off.'

But Haldane was far too eccentric to parody. Sometimes he would stop carving the joint to gaze at its vessels and fibres. Once at dinner he ignored the other guests whilst he pondered a physiological problem. When a cake was brought in for dessert he picked it up without a word and carried it off to his laboratory so he could resume his experiments. On another occasion he arrived home late for dinner having forgotten they were expecting guests. He shot upstairs to change, but didn't return. His wife went to see where he had got to and found him asleep. 'Sorry,' he said. 'I suddenly found myself taking my clothes off and so I thought it must be time for bed.'

In 1906 he turned his attention to the effects of high pressure when asked to investigate the physiology of deep-sea diving. The Admiralty was concerned about the dangers and difficulties of working below 60 feet or so because numerous divers were becoming exhausted, unconscious, paralysed, or worse . . .

Haldane was aided by Dr Teddy Boycott of the Lister Institute in London plus a team of experienced divers from the navy's gunnery and diving School that included Lieutenant Guy Damant and Gunner Catto, whose brother would become the Governor of the Bank of England. In the Royal Navy diving had always been the prerogative of gunners, and Damant 'found going under water a delightful experience and infinitely preferable to the study of ballistics and field-gun drill'. Not all the divers were quite so keen. I have a photograph of one of them standing in that 'I am about to wet my trousers' stance adopted by so many conscripted 'volunteers'.

Preliminary experiments were carried out on goats because they were the only convenient animals close to humans in size. One billy had a taste for consuming coat buttons as well as a watch and several tobacco pouches. It eventually retired to Damant's brother's farm on the Isle of Wight where its horns were gilded in recognition of its stalwart service and, unlike most conscripts, it lived to a ripe old age.

The men were subjected to air compressed to six atmospheres in chambers at the Institute. Haldane seemed to take little interest in the work, but he had already determined what the results would show and was perhaps using the experiments not so much to convince himself, but to show the divers that he knew what he was doing, for their lives were in his hands.

Haldane then decamped to HMS *Spanker* in the Firth of Clyde together with his team and his family. Naomi and Kathleen stayed in a local hotel and explored the brackened hills and vitrified forts, but young Jack was allowed to sleep in a hammock on board the ship in a room lined with rifles.

The divers wore the traditional 'hard hat' diving dress with its metal helmet screwed to the diver's suit. For this, a reliable air supply from the surface was essential: too little air and the diver asphyxiated. The air pressure also protected him from the water pressure outside, as long as they remained the same. If the air supply was cut off and the non-return valve in the helmet failed, the diver had no time to suffocate because he was suddenly and terribly exposed to the water pressure. It was called 'the squeeze'. At depth this meant that his entire body could be rammed up into the helmet, except for the soft bits which would shoot up the air hose.

Too much air was also dangerous, for it inflated the diver's rubber suit and sent him ballooning up to the surface so fast that his lungs also ballooned and exploded. Haldane tackled these problems by inventing the weight belt and binding the legs of the diver's suit so that it couldn't inflate.

The divers were lowered into the sea to almost double the then maximum permitted depth of 100 feet and thereafter the world depth record was broken time after time. They were made to do strenuous exercise while the air they inspired and expired was collected and analysed. The dives passed without incident, except for one. At 180 feet down, Catto attempted to shackle a hawser on to a sinker and became entangled. It was twenty nervous minutes before he could free himself and, as the pump could not supply sufficient air for his exertions, he almost suffocated. He was brought back to the surface just in time.

Haldane recognised that the divers' exhaustion indicated they might be getting too much carbon dioxide, and samples of the air in their helmets on deep dives did indeed contain almost 3 per cent of the gas. But there appeared to be an ample supply of air, certainly enough to sustain the diver in shallower water. However, the ill-effects of breathing 3 per cent carbon dioxide 70 feet down (i.e., at a pressure of over three atmospheres) were equivalent to those of 9 per cent at normal atmospheric pressure. The pumps then in use allowed more than half of the air to leak out past the pistons and were incapable of supplying sufficient air to prevent the build-up of carbon dioxide in the diver's helmet. So Haldane developed the first efficient air pump for deep diving.

By far the most serious danger facing divers was 'compressed air sickness'. After returning to the surface, divers often began vomiting and suffered severe pains in the joints – 'the bends'. Cases of paralysis were common and in the worst cases death ensued. Peter Throckmorton described the bends in Turkish sponge divers: 'If it happens, you can be paralyzed in your sleep, so that you wake up to find yourself a cripple for life. It can choke you to death, kill you instantly, or twist you into a screaming lump of agony with awful pains in your joints. You might get off with only a headache or an itching rash.'

In 1670 Robert Boyle had compressed then decompressed a snake and seen a bubble form in the viper's eye. It was a further two hundred years before Paul Bert's work in France identified the bubble as nitrogen which had dissolved in the body's tissues under pressure and come out of solution when the diver ascended. It was also known that symptoms such as the bends could be relieved by sending the diver back down and renewing the pressure.

To avoid the bends divers were instructed to ascend slowly,

which expended a great deal of time without reliably preventing the symptoms, or to rise cautiously at first then more rapidly as they neared the surface – the exact opposite of what they needed to do. Haldane's results showed that the danger of decompressing lay entirely in the last stages on approaching the surface. The weight of water pressing in on the diver 33 feet down is equivalent to that of the atmosphere that stretches for miles above our heads. Thus, in ascending to the surface from 33 feet, he halves the pressure from two atmospheres to one, but if he is twice as deep (66 feet down) the pressure is not doubled again, for he is now at only three atmospheres. If he were 200 feet down, he would have to rise over 100 feet before the pressure was halved.

Haldane argued that since the bends had never occurred when a diver had risen rapidly from a depth of 33 feet to the surface, thus halving the pressure, it should also be safe to decompress from four atmospheres to two or from six to three. So it proved.

He was able to calculate a system of staged decompression in which the diver came up rapidly to the depth at which the pressure was halved, then rose in stages designed to ensure that the pressure of nitrogen in the body never became more than about twice that of the air breathed. These first decompression tables allowed for the maximum depth to which the diver had descended and the time spent there. The tables published in 1907 were universally accepted, and were used until superseded in 1956. The 'Haldane concepts' remain the basis for all tables devised since. No development in the history of diving has saved so many lives. The Admiralty's gratitude took the form of a visit to a silver-smith's for Mrs Haldane to choose a coffee pot, candlesticks and an engraved salver.

Haldane emphasised that the rate of nitrogen saturation

varied considerably in different parts of the body. Most tissues absorb about 70 per cent more than the blood; thus the white tissue in the central nervous system has very little blood supply and a high capacity for storing nitrogen. Nitrogen is also about six times more soluble in body fats than in blood and it is nitrogen bubbles in the fatty sheaths around nerves that cause the pain of the bends. From the experiments with goats in the pressure chambers, Damant demonstrated that fat animals were more susceptible to compressed air sickness than slim ones and needed to decompress for longer. The team went on to investigate the effects of chronic exposure to high pressure as experienced by tunnellers working in caissons, pressurised underwater cabins.

Already an authority on respiration at high pressures, Haldane now turned his attention to the effects of high altitudes and low pressures. Mountain sickness in climbers was known to result from the decreased pressure of oxygen at high altitude, but the invention of the aeroplane and the possible danger to pilots flying at ever greater heights sent physiologists scurrying up mountains to conduct experiments. At a conference, Haldane casually hinted that if only there were a high mountain with a decent hotel on top he would investigate changes in the blood and respiration that occurred at altitude. Taking him at his word, a physiologist from Yale hauled him to over 14,000 feet on Pike's Peak in Colorado for five weeks to study acclimatisation to oxygen deficiency. As they became used to the altitude, they maliciously enjoyed the sight of tourists disembarking from the mountain railway and immediately succumbing to mountain sickness. Athletes who have benefited from altitude training have Haldane to thank for our understanding of the physiological changes they undergo.

*

Haldane's main claim to scientific fame is his discovery that it is the accumulation of carbon dioxide in the lungs and consequently in the blood that governs breathing. In animals at rest, breathing is regulated so as to control the amount of carbon dioxide in the lungs. Even tiny changes in the carbon dioxide concentration of the blood passing from the lungs to the brain cause very large changes in the breathing rate. These results revolutionised physiology by supplying a coherent explanation of the natural changes in breathing that accompany variations in physical activity. He also showed that chemical changes in the blood could bring about quantitative changes in different parts of the body with astonishing sensitivity and precision. Physiologists realised for the first time that chemical control was as important as nervous control.

Haldane also invented several tests and pieces of analytical equipment that allowed physiologists to do things that were impossible before. His gas analysis apparatus, for example, enabled the entire volume of blood in an animal's body to be estimated from a tiny blood sample.

In later life Haldane became increasingly interested in philosophy and the role of science in what he believed to be a spiritual world. He was the epitome of the gentleman scientist, kindly and humanitarian and, of course, absent-minded. No wonder he was appalled at the behaviour of the 'Bloods' in college, gangs of anti-intellectual upper-class vandals who caused havoc by breaking into laboratories, tearing up books of results and dunking academics in baths of mercury. But the Great War would soon sweep away the Philistines as well as the poets.

In 1915 at the request of his brother, Richard, now Lord Chancellor, Haldane was charged with identifying the poison gas being used by the Germans, and to devise some protection for the troops in the trenches. He rushed to France to attend the post mortem of a victim of the first gas attack, a young Canadian officer killed by inhaling chlorine. Haldane was furious when Kitchener entreated British mothers to make (ineffectual) gas masks for the troops. It was just a ploy to distract an anxious populace and make them feel that they were doing something to help.

Haldane's house now echoed with the sound of coughing and retching from the attic, signifying that the experiments were progressing well. Father and son were breathing toxic gases and testing gas masks of their own design. Before they succeeded, Haldane's lungs had been damaged and would complain for the remainder of his life. Naomi and Aldous Huxley shredded woollens to provide the absorbent filling for the respirators. They tried stockings, vests, Naomi's knitted cap and Aldous' scarf before they got it right and produced the first effective gas masks.

Haldane still gave occasional lectures and attended seminars at the college. Naomi often accompanied him, with instructions to dig him in the ribs if he fell 'too obviously asleep'.

At the age of seventy-five, having just returned from investigating heat stroke in oil-rig workers in the Middle East, he collapsed and developed pneumonia. His lungs had never recovered from the experiments on poison gases and his heart was worn out.

His failing mind swirled with thoughts, some concerning his collaborators. His last words were, 'I've had a telegram to say that Priestley was dying too, but I think it was an imaginary telegram.' He died in an oxygen tent as the clock struck midnight, with 'a look of intense interest on his face as though he were taking part in some crucial experiment in physiology which had to be carefully monitored'.

The Oxford Department of Anatomy, to whom he had willed his body, asked to be freed from the obligation to dissect a friend and colleague. So he was cremated and his ashes scattered at the family graveyard at the mouth of Gleneagles. Ripples of consternation spread throughout the family when Jack, 'in the full tide of communist conversion', insisted on bringing up the ashes by train – third-class and on the overhead luggage rack.

John Haldane remained a powerful figure in the lives of his children. Years after his death, he still came to Naomi's dreams as 'the area of safety, occasionally as the exorciser, or perhaps the explainer who makes it quite clear that as a matter of fact and once one grasps the pattern of what it is all about, everything is perfectly all right . . . In these reassuring dreams it is always my father, never my mother, once the childhood dispenser of safety and reassurance.'

Haldane left two legacies to science. One was the new direction he had given to the study of human physiology and the other was his son, who would also make a major contribution to our knowledge of the physiology of divers.

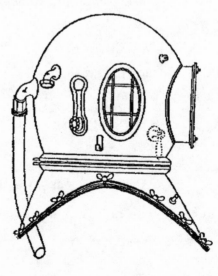

Hard-hat helmet from Haldane and Priestley's classic 1935 book, *Respiration*
(*By permission of Oxford University Press*)

J. B. S. at work in the laboratory at Cambridge in the early 1920s
(*By permission of the Colman Library, Department of Biochemistry, University of Cambridge, England*)

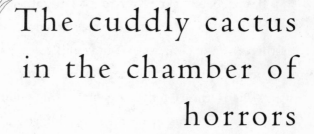

The cuddly cactus in the chamber of horrors

John Burdon Sanderson Haldane
1892–1964

Haldane's son, Jack (universally known as J. B. S.), was the greatest mind to interest itself in diving. He was born on Guy Fawkes night and there would be fireworks wherever he went.

He was a remarkable child. When his father was discussing blood, three-year-old Jack became impatient. 'But is it oxyhaemoglobin or carboxyhaemoglobin?' he asked. Just before his fifth birthday he was expected to read out the newspaper reports of the meetings of the British Association. By five he had read *Gulliver's Travels*, and, although he was too young to study Latin, he passed the examination. 'I know you didn't teach it to me,' he explained to the master, 'but I heard you all the same.'

It was an unusual upbringing. At the age of seven he made a collection of sea shells and when he asked his father to help identify them he was handed a two-volume treatise in German. By eight he was trusted to note down the readings his father called out when using his gas analysis apparatus and soon he was calculating all the data from the experiments. On one expedition a few years later, his father realised they had forgotten to bring log tables. 'Never mind,' he said, 'Jack will calculate a set for us.'

When being taken for a ride on his father's bicycle he fell off and fractured his skull. It was touch and go. If he were to die, his mother made it clear, she would hold John responsible. After a long period of unconsciousness, Jack recovered and was soon alert again. On overhearing the surgeon recommending the dosage of a drug, he opened his eyes and said, 'But you are the mechanical chap, leave that to the chemical chap.'

With his sister, Naomi, he laid out trails of gunpowder and lit them to good effect, singeing her eyebrows. They gutted one of her dolls for anatomical interest and skinned a woolly caterpillar to make a fur rug for her doll's house. He also terrified her with something that glinted in a dark cupboard, which he swore was radium. Jack was full of good ideas. He put a dummy head in bed beside his sister so that she would awaken with a scream. He ran cables from the electric socket into the wash-hand basin, then threw pennies into the water for Naomi to pluck out at her peril. To pep up the housemaid he also wired up the washboard.

During his first eighteen months at Eton it was his turn to be teased and tortured by the older boys. Jack hated school but was later immune from bullying by virtue of his formidable size and aggressive disposition. His pugnaciousness would serve him well in later battles against authority and government, and the isolation from his fellow pupils that his brilliance and arrogance conferred on him at school enabled him to identify with the exploited masses whose cause he would champion for the rest of his life.

In 1908 his father was invited by the Admiralty to take part in the trials of a new type of submarine, and he needed an assistant. The choice was limited by the Official Secrets Act. 'Why not take the boy?' said his wife. He turned to Jack and asked, 'What's the formula for soda-lime?' Jack immediately recited the correct formula and the next thing he knew he was in a top secret submarine.

He first dived, down to 36 feet, in hard-hat gear when only thirteen years old. 'My ears pained,' he admitted, 'but they didn't burst.' The suit was of course far too large and the cuffs too wide. It rapidly filled with water so the lad calmly twiddled the air valves and managed to keep the water level just below his chin. Even then he was fearless and cool under pressure.

At nineteen he published his first scientific paper, jointly with his father, and went up to Oxford to study mathematics, although he soon switched to a more respectable subject, classics. To the end of his life, a little alcohol would unlock acres of verse. He would often drop in uninvited on Julian Huxley, usually at tea-time and 'devour plates of biscuits, protesting that he couldn't eat a crumb, while reciting Shelley or Milton and any other poet you chose, by the yard . . . Once he went on reciting Homer so long that I had to escort him, spouting Greek all the time, downstairs to the front door.'

Jack was in his element. He became an expert climber so that he could enter or leave college after hours by scaling the walls. Years later, when he returned as a don, he closed most of the easier routes so as to improve the standard of midnight mountaineering.

The warden of Hall was an unctuous albino called Spooner. Not all his spoonerisms were authentic, but when the college cat fell from a window and escaped unharmed, he reassured colleagues with 'She popped on her drawers and away she went.' At such moments his formidable wife would fix the students with her stony look and dare them to smile.

Jack took a year out to read zoology and, although he never took a degree in biology, he had already started experimental studies in genetics. At home the bathroom became cluttered with bowls of sand-hoppers and the front garden was given over to the rearing of guinea-pigs and mice. They were each named after a prominent scientist and tended by Naomi and Aldous Huxley, who was now part of the household. Jack kept records of the inheritance of various traits such as pelt colour. The resultant publication was the first report of linkage (two or more characters being inherited together) in vertebrates.

The award of a first-class degree in classics in August 1914 was, Jack admitted, 'somewhat overshadowed by other events'. Bombing officer Haldane of the Black Watch found the war 'a very enjoyable experience'. April 1915 – 'one of the happiest months of my life' – was spent under constant bombardment. Field Marshal Haig described him as 'the bravest and dirtiest officer in the army'.

He relished night-time forays into no man's land to eaves-drop on enemy troops or give them a fright. His exploits became legendary and Naomi described him as 'a killer silently getting to the enormously dangerous but only correct spot from which to lob his bomb into the enemy trench'. He admitted that he enjoyed the opportunity of killing people as it was a 'respectable relic of primitive man'. So was being killed, of course. Once, in daylight, he cycled across a gap in full view of the Germans in the belief, fortunately correct, that they would be too surprised to open fire before he made cover. He called it 'taking a novel risk, which you are not ordered to take . . . and enjoying it'. Not surprisingly he was seriously wounded twice, the second time by what is now affectionately known as 'friendly fire'. Luckily he was picked up by the Prince of Wales and taken to a dressing station. Had he not been temporarily seconded to work with his father on the development of the gas mask, he would have taken part in the suicidal charge at Richebourg L'Avoué in which almost every officer in his battalion was killed.

His next task was to organise a bombing school. 'I began by lecturing on the anatomy of hand grenades and made each pupil attach a detonator to a fuse with his teeth.' He explained that 'should the detonator explode . . . the mouth would be considerably enlarged. Pupils who did not show alacrity when confronted with this . . . were returned to duty as unlikely to become efficient instructors.' Among their other antics was to play catch with lighted bombs before throwing them out of the trench. 'Provided you are a good judge of time, it is no more dangerous than crossing the road . . . but it is much more impressive to onlookers.' Although there were no casualties, 'some idiot asked questions about it in parliament, and got an army order issued forbidding the practice.'

He habitually carried a pocketful of detonators, gelignite and loose matches and would 'at the slightest provocation, expound upon their use'. Understandably, he was viewed with 'suspicion and fear' by his fellow officers, especially when he tamped down his glowing pipe with a detonator whilst lecturing them on how easily accidents can happen. It goes without saying that he loved bonfires and fireworks and never blew out a match until it had burnt down to his fingers.

After the war he returned to Oxford and then moved on to Cambridge where he began the physiological work with himself and his colleagues as guinea-pigs, which would occupy him for the next sixteen years. The early experiments involved swallowing bicarbonate of soda and then hydrochloric acid to examine the acidity of the blood. 'Concentrated HCl dissolves one's teeth,' he noted. 'The strongest I ever cared to drink was about one part in a hundred of water, but a pint was enough for me as it irritated my throat and stomach.' Unfortunately, his calculations showed that he needed a gallon and a half to get the effect he wanted. He tried smuggling the acid into his body under false pretences by taking a compound that would be broken down internally to liberate acid. It worked, although he admitted that his liver 'would have resembled a Seidlitz powder, but even had I had a window through which to watch the process I should have been too busy breathing to pay much attention'. He suffered severe symptoms of acid poisoning. A colleague found him 'drunk' on the stairs and rushed to his aid. 'It's nothing,' Haldane assured him. 'It's just that I'm only 80 per cent sodium haldanate at the present moment.' The technique was later used to treat babies who suffered tetanus caused by excessively alkaline blood.

Haldane's reasons for conducting experiments on himself were that a rabbit could not tell you how it felt and 'made no serious attempt to co-operate with one'. Also, 'to do the same sort of things to a dog . . . requires a licence signed in triplicate by two archbishops.'

Haldane was meticulous in his experiments but clumsy at everything else. In the most decrepit car Arthur C. Clarke had ever seen, he drove with 'fearless abandon, little skill and old-world courtesy, up the Tooting Road, missing bollards, policemen etc. by a hair's breadth'. He also retained a childish sense of humour and fearlessly broached taboo subjects in a loud voice in public. He was famous for clearing a Lyons tea shop of sensitive ladies.

Aldous Huxley mercilessly lampooned him in the novel, *Antic Hay*. The ponderous physiologist, James Shearwater, spends hours on an exercise bicycle in a 'Hot Box' with sweat dripping from his moustache, travelling seventy miles a day without going anywhere at all. When accused of seeming uninterested in female company, he admits to allocating only half an hour per day to women, including his wife. 'I know all about love already,' he claims, and presents a mathematical equation to prove it. 'I am quietly married, I simmer away domestically.' Meanwhile, his wife was coming to the boil. Whilst he discusses germ plasm in the parlour below, she is being tupped by a stranger upstairs.

In 1923 Haldane published his prophesies on the future of science. His imaginings on eugenics and test-tube babies were sensational:

> It was in 1951 that Dupont and Schwarz . . . obtained a fresh ovary from a woman who was the victim of an aeroplane accident, and kept it living in their medium for five years . . . Now that the technique is fully developed, we can take an ovary from a woman and keep it growing in seminal fluid for as long as twenty years, producing a fresh ovum each month, of which 90 per cent can be fertilised, and the embryos grown successfully for nine months, and then brought out into the air. France was the first country to adopt ectogenesis [external birth] officially, and by 1968 was producing 60,000 children annually by this method.
>
> As we know, ectogenesis is now universal, and in this country less than 30 per cent of children are now born to woman.

Aldous Huxley was fascinated by Haldane's ideas and used them as the basis for *Brave New World*.

Haldane believed there were three great dangers to the world: communism, fascism and journalism. Then he met

Charlotte Burghes, a communist who wrote for the *Daily Express*. 'Teaching was J. B. S.'s supreme hobby,' she wrote, 'and learning was mine . . . we met more and more regularly. He lectured, I listened . . . and when, with a charming affectation of eighteenth-century gallantry, he implored my favours, I did not withhold them.' She was a married woman so, according to the custom of the day, they contrived a tryst in a hotel to supply grounds for a divorce. Although they married in 1926, a university committee (with the sinister name, Sex Viri – the six men) found Haldane guilty of 'gross habitual immorality' and stripped him of his readership. He refused to resign and won an appeal, thus emasculating the 'Sex Weary' committee for ever.

Charlotte became his secretary and agent and sold his articles. He was always writing; in trains or airport lounges he could be seen scribbling away. Not a moment was wasted. He would eventually pen twenty-three books and over four hundred scientific papers.

In 1928 they visited Russia and were impressed with the esteem enjoyed there by scientists. Jack became a confirmed Marxist. He was attracted by the seductive socialist notion that science should be of practical use to the common man rather than the esoteric philosophy of a few. Although a subsequent visit disabused him of the virtues of Stalinism, his Marxist beliefs were reinforced by the tolerance of the British government towards fascist dictators.

His socialism and atheism are summed up in his claim that 'Between 3000 BC and AD 1400 there were probably only four really important inventions, namely the general use of iron, paved roads, voting, and religious intolerance.'

When asked what his studies had told him about God, he famously replied, 'that he has an inordinate fondness for beetles'.

He supplemented Blake's line on the tiger, 'Did he who made the Lamb make thee?', with: 'The same question applies with equal force to the tapeworm, and an affirmative answer would clearly postulate a creator whose sense of values would not commend him to the admiration of society.'

In 1933 he moved to University College, London, first as Professor of Genetics and then to the Chair of Biometry. In the next few years Hitler unwittingly staffed Haldane's department with a stream of gifted Jewish biologists fleeing from the Continent. He introduced Ernst Chain to Howard Florey and together they would purify penicillin to make the first practical antibiotic, for which they received the Nobel prize.

Most of Haldane's work was theoretical, applying mathematics to data collected by others. Equations were applied to genetics, including human inheritance of colour-blindness and haemophilia. He was the first to begin to map the genes on a human chromosome and to estimate the rate of genetic change in a human gene. Surprisingly, he found that it was the *rate* of mutation more than the adverse effects of any individual change that determined the influence of harmful mutations on the population. It was as if the degree of drunkenness was influenced more by the speed of drinking than by the amount of alcohol swallowed. He also began to quantify the mechanisms of evolution, to show that Darwin's theory of natural selection could not just cause change, but that the rate of change was sufficient to account for the speed of evolution. His book, *The Causes of Evolution*, remains a classic. Almost single-handedly he laid the foundations of both human genetics and population genetics. He not only designed the tools, but honed them for others to use.

During the Spanish civil war, Charlotte worked in a transit camp in France from which volunteers for the International

Brigade were kitted out and smuggled into Spain. Haldane advised the Spanish government on how to cope with gas attacks and bombing raids.

During an air raid in Madrid he didn't run for cover; nor did the woman sitting beside him in the park. When a bomb exploded nearby she was killed instantly by shrapnel. He was unharmed, but chronically shaken. Walking the Scottish hills with his sister three years later, 'he looked about him for cover as soon as he stopped, doing it almost instinctively.'

In 1938 Jack was elected a Fellow of the Royal Society. He was forty-six years old, bald, with twinkling eyes and a large moustache, with the air of a mischievous walrus. He was wonderful with children, but often uneasy with adults. They were awed by his brilliance and his peculiar formal manners. When someone entered the room he would rise, stride forward and bow 'like a performing hippopotamus'. His sister observed that 'He has the mannerisms of the great, but I suspect that underneath he doesn't feel at all at his ease or grown-up. At any moment, he feels . . . someone may come and send him up to bed.'

As science correspondent for the communist newspaper, *The Daily Worker*, for thirteen years, he produced almost 350 articles, all beautifully clear, succinct accounts of scientific topics, laced with a socialist moral. He saw the articles as part of his duty as a biologist: 'The enemies of science alternately abuse its exponents for being deaf to moral considerations and for interfering in ethical problems which do not concern them. Both of these criticisms cannot be right.'

His mission was to apply biology and social engineering for the betterment of mankind; after all, 'The great majority of us are quite capable of some kind of useful acitivity. The essential social problems of today, as they present themselves to a biologist, are to determine the abilities of different people, and to organise society so that the demand for various kinds of human ability should equal the supply.'

Haldane was the finest popular science writer of his generation and was master of the vivid analogy. When discussing the power-to-weight ratio necessary for flight he mentions that 'An angel whose muscles developed no more power weight for weight than those of an eagle or a pigeon would require a breast projecting for about four feet to house the muscles engaged in working its wings, while to economise in weight, its legs would have to be reduced to mere stilts.' Furthermore, the giants in *The Pilgrim's Progress* could not possibly look like the illustration in the book for, if of the same proportions as a normal-sized man, they would, for mechanical reasons, have broken their thigh bones every time they took a step. 'This was doubtless why they were sitting down in the picture I remember. But it lessens one's respect for Christian and Jack the Giant Killer.'

He then turned his lively mind to the problems of the looming conflict with Nazi Germany. In Madrid he had spent his time minutely recording the results of air raids, what gave protection and what did not. He saw the potential mortality from bomb damage as a statistical problem and published an article on the mathematics of air-raid protection, as well as a practical guide to air-raid precautions that sold well at the time of the Munich crisis. He tried in vain to persuade the British government of the value of deep shelters. To prove the inadequacy of the flimsy, above-ground Anderson shelters, he offered to sit in one whilst explosives were detonated closer and closer. The government paid no attention and Haldane called their policy 'London unprotected'. Fortunately, when air raids began, Londoners broke into the Underground stations and used them as deep shelters.

Haldane had tried to warn the government about the potentially destructive power of atomic bombs and would later play a major role in evaluating the genetic damage caused by radiation, estimating that the amount of exposure that would double the natural mutation rate in humans might be only one twentieth of that assumed at the time.

He put forward wondrous schemes to allow frogmen to cross fast-flowing rivers and for the release of thousands of fish tagged with tiny magnets to trigger magnetic mines, but his moment came three months before war erupted, when the submarine HMS *Thetis* sank during trials in Liverpool Bay, having dived with both ends of its torpedo tubes open. Even though the vessel was intact with its stern protruding from the water, only four of the 108 men on board survived. Rightly fearing that there was no help available at the surface, the crew left it too late to escape. Almost half of the victims were civilian mechanics, and the trades unions asked Haldane to represent their interests at the public enquiry.

Haldane and a couple of friends locked themselves in a steel chamber at the Siebe Gorman factory in London to simulate the effects of incarceration in a disabled submarine. They remained there for fourteen and a half hours and, as the carbon dioxide concentration rose, became too sick and incapacitated to put on the Davis submarine escape gear. Haldane vomited up a pint of clear fluid, not having eaten during the ordeal in order to parallel the conditions in the *Thetis*. He clearly stated the problem of escaping from disabled submarines at depth as how to steer 'between the Scylla of nitrogen poisoning and "bends" and the Charybdis of oxygen poisoning'.

It brought home to him the terror of being trapped under water. Haldane confided to his sister how terrible it must have been for some of the *Thetis'* crew to be in the escape chamber with the water rising, unable to get the hatch open. He wouldn't advise anyone to go in submarines, 'those bloody awful machines, all the human ingenuity . . . going into that. I am quite unable to be anything but anti-war.' He later channelled this into the belief that 'It would be well if physiologists were to investigate the effect of abnormal conditions on human beings, *before* these conditions have killed numerous people.'

He convinced the Admiralty that to increase the chances of submariners surviving in a disabled submarine, what was needed was a thorough investigation of how people reacted when breathing a deteriorating atmosphere under pressure. They agreed to sponsor the work and he became one of the few card-carrying communists to carry out secret military research on behalf of the British government. In 1940 he was chairman of the editorial board of the *Daily Worker* when the paper was banned, but was also advising the War Office on anti-invasion plans. He would eventually resign from the communist party, not because his socialist zeal had waned, but over Russia's devotion to the 'politically correct' but totally spurious genetics of Lysenko and the manner in which its critics were ruthlessly eradicated.

He gathered a group of collaborators including Dr Juan Negrín, a former prime minister of Spain, four members of the International Brigade (because they would be cool under pressure), his secretary, and a bright young research student, Helen Spurway. All of them were the experimental subjects and were tested, if not to destruction, then at least to unconsciousness. Almost every experiment ended with someone having a seizure, bleeding or vomiting. 'Good,' Haldane would say, 'that's another point on the graph.' Nose bleeds were so common that a colleague claimed: 'We could usually track down the Professor . . .

by following the trail of bloody handkerchiefs.'

The experiments were conducted in a 'pressure pot', a steel chamber like a boiler on its side, measuring eight feet long by four in diameter. Two or three people could sit in one, but they couldn't begin to stand up. The 'rabbits' had no telephone, so they communicated with the exterior by tapping in code or holding up messages to the small window.

One chamber was large enough to be flooded to a depth of over seven feet so that some strenuous tests could be carried out under water with an attendant sitting on a shelf just above the surface ready to retrieve the diver when he passed out. High pressure and low temperatures were a deadly combination. When clad only in shirt and slacks, immersed in a bath of melting ice and breathing an aberrant atmosphere at a pressure ten times greater than normal, unconsciousness came mercifully soon. Even

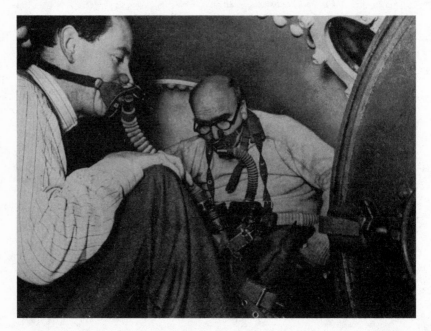

J. B. S. (right) with Martin Case in the 'Chamber of Horrors', ca. 1940
(*From the Siebe Gorman archive by permission of Siebe plc*)

hardened divers got severe claustrophobia in this tank. Haldane admitted that 'since these experiments are extremely uncomfortable, I have unfortunately not been able to confirm my observations by those of other experimenters.'

Haldane described what it was like to be a rabbit in the chamber:

> I am breathing rapidly and deeply and my pulse is 110 . . . soon I feel much better, though perhaps my writing is a little wobbly. But why cannot my companion behave himself? He is making silly jokes and trying to sing. His lips are rather purple, the colour of haemoglobin when uncombined with oxygen. I feel quite unaffected; in fact I have just thought of a very funny story. It is true I can't stand without support. My companion suggests some oxygen from the cylinder . . . To humour him I take a few breaths. The result is startling. The electric light becomes so much brighter that I fear the fuse will melt. The noise of the pump increases fourfold. My note-book, which should have contained records of my pulse rate, turns out to be filled with the often repeated but seldom legible statement that I am feeling *much* better, and remarks about my colleague, of which the least libellous is that he is drunk. I put down the oxygen tube and relapse into a not unpleasant state of mental confusion.

As a result of these experiments, Haldane boasted, 'I probably hold the world record of one and a half hours' continuous spasm of the hands and face.'

Haldane's father called the pressure pot 'the chamber of horrors'. It is easy to see why.

During compression it became warm in the chamber, as a bicycle pump warms when you inflate the tyres. Haldane fanned himself with a folded newspaper, but it tore to shreds in air so dense that bluebottles were unable to fly. When decompressing, the cooling damp air filled the chamber with fog. After a few weeks Haldane's wristwatch ground to a halt under the weight of rust on the mainspring. He bought an air-tight watch – and it crumpled the first time he compressed.

The speed at which they changed pressure sometimes caused problems. Haldane's fastest 'dive' was from one to seven atmospheres in 90 seconds, experiencing the pressure changes of a pilot diving vertically at twice the speed of sound. Rapid 'ascents' were more dangerous, causing one of his filled teeth to emit a high-pitched scream and explode because of an air pocket that couldn't vent fast enough. A colleague had one side of his lung collapse on several occasions. If both had gone, he would have died.

Minor bends were commonplace. Haldane was partially paralysed in his left buttock, but felt fortunate that 'it wasn't in a more important sensory region'. He also burst both his eardrums. They healed, leaving small holes in the membranes. It made him slightly deaf, a small price to pay for the ability to blow smoke rings through his ears – a skill Jack Kitching saw him exhibit at a party.

Among the numerous phenomena investigated systematically for the first time was nitrogen narcosis. Breathing pressurised air, which is mostly nitrogen, induces intoxication as effectively as alcohol. Helen Spurway described its effects at pressures equivalent to a depth of 300 feet: 'My fingers felt like bananas' and

fanning 'makes me feel hyper . . . hyper-op-hera-tera-herea.'
When under pressure, a distinguished Fellow of the Royal
Society tried to multiply two four-figure sums, but put down only
two numbers in five minutes, one of which was wrong, and
declared: 'It's a bloody silly test.' As soon as he switched from
breathing compressed air to a helium-oxygen mixture he recovered his wits and solved the sums in his head. Only Helen's
maths improved under pressure.

His attraction towards Helen was also putting pressure on
his marriage, which was beginning to founder. There were many
disagreements, mostly over matters of principle. Charlotte found
the blitz 'thrilling and exciting and . . . the fires, in themselves,
intensely beautiful' and, while J. B. S. sheltered in the basement,
she stayed in the drawing room above and played the Bechstein,
'to drown the noise of the guns', or even went out in the car to get
a closer look at the flames. One night he insisted that they take
cover in the public air-raid shelter nearby. That very night it was
hit by a bomb and a woman died. Thereafter, Charlotte stayed at
home, and he took shelter in the office basement at Regents Park
Zoo where Julian Huxley was the director. That too was bombed,
but the fires were extinguished with water from the sea lion pond.

Haldane fully appreciated the potential of using helium–
oxygen, now universally adopted for deep diving. He had experi-
mented with it in 1943 after an American company claimed it was
less likely than air to cause the bends. Using tables safe for normal decompression resulted in a helium bubble in his spine,
which caused him discomfort throughout his life and made him
'sceptical of American salesmanship'. But in true Haldane fashion,
he learned 'to ignore certain types of sensory input'.

At that time working at pressures equivalent to depths of
200 feet called for exceptional skill and technical capability.

'Dives' to 400 feet achieved by Haldane's team approached the record depths then conceivable.

All the experiments were supervised by a tester inside the chamber, but the tester often became as intoxicated as the testee and forgot to time the trial or to take proper notes.

The research led to modifications to the procedures for escaping from submarines and established 220 feet as the lower limit for the safe use of compressed air. Below this depth nitrogen intoxication can be so severe that a diver may offer his air supply to a passing fish, under the impression that it is drowning.

Wartime brought new problems and a new urgency to solve them. Frogmen and underwater charioteers used oxygen rebreathing apparatus as it does not release tell-tale bubbles, so the team also investigated the effects of oxygen under pressure. There followed the most exhaustive programme of diving experiments ever attempted – more than 1,000 dives in toxic conditions to depths of 90 feet. To their surprise, they found that the odourless and tasteless gas that supported all life on the planet tasted like stale ginger beer and was toxic under pressure, causing convulsions violent enough to break a bone. Haldane suffered crushed vertebrae and a dislocated hip from a sudden muscular contraction. Of particular danger was the unpredictability of the seizure; on one occasion Helen lasted 85 minutes at a pressure of three atmospheres, on another only 13 minutes. Haldane was at first more resistant than most, but after about a hundred experiments, he became so sensitive that he began to twitch violently after only five minutes' exposure to oxygen. They established that breathing pure oxygen was dangerous below thirty feet.

Later, when the Admiralty reintroduced miniature submarines, they asked Haldane to see if it was safe for the diver to leave a submerged vessel to plant a mine on a ship's hull and then re-enter the submarine. He and his most stalwart collaborator, Martin Case, incarcerated themselves in a mock steel submarine on the bottom of Portsmouth harbour, 'screwed up like so much shrimp paste in a jar'. As the tank was being lowered into the water the crane driver ran for cover and left them dangling in mid-air throughout an air raid. They stayed locked in the submerged sub for two days continuously with the light and telephone links working only intermittently. A ship passed too close overhead and the tank was torn from its moorings, shaking up the prisoners inside. They concluded that with one cylinder of oxygen the crew could live comfortably for three days and stay submerged 'without serious loss of efficiency, for twelve hours without any reconditioning of the air'.

Haldane's idea of comfort was, of course, not quite the same as yours or mine. Later he exposed himself to a pressure of ten atmospheres and then plunged into water at zero degrees Celsius as an undress rehearsal for going for a sub-sea stroll in Arctic waters. These experiments paved the way for the successful raid on the battleship *Tirpitz*.

In 1943 the War Office anticipated that, come D-Day, frogmen would be expected to clear mines and shore defences. The divers might have to surface quickly to avoid underwater explosions, which are dangerous over a much greater distance than terrestrial ones. If they breathed a mixture of air and oxygen they would take in far less nitrogen and could therefore come up faster. The trick was to get the proportions right; too much air and they would get the bends, too much oxygen and they would suffer fits. So Haldane and Helen were compressed to the equivalent of 70 feet down and tried out various gas mixtures. If either of them got the bends, then they would take a day off to allow the nitrogen to clear their system. They showed that a surfacing procedure, which according to the tables should take forty-seven minutes, could be done safely in two. This gas mixture was used in 1944 by the 'P-Parties' that cleared occupied ports.

Haldane suggested that animals could be induced to 'breathe' oxygenated liquids rather than air. Much later the US navy showed that this was possible, in experiments aimed at eliminating the troublesome compressible gases from deep-diving experiments.

His only honour for all his war work was to be included in the Nazis' list of those to be arrested when England was invaded.

There were, however, greater conflicts than just the war. University College locked out of their laboratories those scientists that were seconded on war work. One colleague resorted to fisticuffs with the Dean. J. B S. was turgid with envy.

In 1945, as soon as his divorce from Charlotte became final, he married Helen Spurway. Haldane made friends and enemies with equal facility. Warm yet irascible, 'a cuddly cactus' a friend called him, he possessed the regal rudeness of Conan Doyle's Professor Challenger, although this was usually directed at strangers, and especially journalists, rather than colleagues. But for all his kindness and concern for allies, there was always a certain aloofness, an apartness about him. His first wife recounted a time when it began to hail during a bull fight. Everyone fled except for Haldane. He sat alone in the pelting rain with a mac over his head quietly smoking his pipe. The only other creature present was an abandoned bull alone in the ring.

He continually fought with the university authorities. In 1957 his patience ran out and he and Helen moved to the Statistical Institute in Calcutta (and later to his own institute), declaring: 'Climate grand, living cheap, great demand for teachers.' In any case, 'sixty years in socks is quite enough.'

He fell in love with the country, adopted Indian dress and food and studied Hindu philosophy. At night he would sit on the flat roof of his house and discourse on the stars, or swim in a water tank in the garden with smooth, cool fish flapping against his legs and just his head protruding above the surface, preceded by the glow from a large cigar or the diver's helmet bowl of his Siebe Gorman pipe.

He devoted much of his energy to encouraging talented young Indian biologists and was generous with his time and money. If funded to travel first-class he chose economy and used the difference to pay for his students to go too. The fees from his popular articles funded their projects. He was never dogmatic and

J. B. S. in Indian dress and in need of an iron, 1961
(*By permission of SOLO Syndication Ltd.*)

always enthusiastic about their research, and had only two bits of advice for them: 'Keep your eyes open and expect the unexpected.' Coffee breaks were a delight in the presence of probably the most erudite scientist of the century. His stories, on any subject, were 'masterpieces of intelligence and humour'. A student asked him, 'Do you have to have the skin of a rhino to achieve success in public life?' 'No,' he replied, 'you need the *brain* of a rhino.'

When seventy-one years old he dived for the last time. Taken to see a coral reef, he declared: 'The only place to see fish is underwater', and promptly stripped off and dived in.

But the idyll was not to last. In 1964 he was diagnosed as having a malignant tumour in his rectum. After it was removed he wrote, 'These events lead me to attend rather more closely . . . to the fact that I shall die within a few years.' He even wrote a poem to his tumour called *Cancer's a Funny Thing*:

> I wish I had the voice of Homer
> To sing of rectal carcinoma . . .
> I asked a doctor, now a friend,
> To peer into my hinder end . . .
> The microscope returned the answer
> That I had certainly got cancer.
> So I was wheeled into the theatre
> Where holes were made to make me better . . .
> So now I am like two-faced Janus
> The only god who sees his anus . . .
> So do not wait for aches and pains
> To have a surgeon mend your drains . . .
> For if you wait it's sure to swell,
> And may have progeny as well . . .
> Provided one confronts the tumour

With a sufficient sense of humour . . .
A spot of laughter, I am sure,
Often accelerates one's cure

Hundreds of letters arrived, half of them commending his courage and the rest condemning his candour.

'The valiant never taste of death but once,' he wrote, but 'one only becomes valiant by sipping this taste . . . by flirting with death.' Haldane pictured death as a woman who 'without wishing to go all the way, [is] prepared to do so when the occasion arises'. He was content to die in peace 'on an easy chair . . . on my veranda, looking at flowering trees and birds in the sunshine'. He had no desire to be born again: 'I would prefer to be replaced by someone without some of my congenital deficiencies.'

'The one thing I am really sorry to have missed is walking to France on the sea bottom, which incidentally would have involved some interesting physiological research beforehand. Sadly, I only got the money needed for this purpose at the age of seventy.' But he had enjoyed the magic of being alive. 'I have tried morphine, heroin and bhang and ganja. The alterations of my consciousness due to these drugs were trivial compared with those produced in the course of my work . . . I have had the standard adventurous experiences such as being pulled out of a crevasse in a glacier, and more which are unusual . . . I doubt I should have found many greater thrills in a hundred lives.'

He knew that he 'might die within a year if the cancer has sent a colony of cells to another part of my body, perhaps twenty-five if it has not'. Unfortunately it had, and within a few months science had lost one of its most gifted and courageous spirits. He left his body for medical research and teaching, adding that it 'has been used for both purposes during my lifetime'.

Wright in his beloved Alpha Romeo

Boom!

Horace Cameron Wright 1901?–1979

Some scientists, like the Haldanes, become famous, but most do not. A public familiar with every witless socialite would be hard-pressed to name even the most distinguished physiologist. During the war and the Cold War that followed, there was a hidden army of back-room boffins fighting the enemy with their intellect and often with their personal courage too. One of these was Cam Wright.

He produced twenty-five research reports all of which were classified as secret and never released. The Defence Research Information Centre has no copies and no idea what happened to them. Apart from brief mentions in the technical reports of others, Wright remains unknown except to his old friends and colleagues. It is from their recollections that I have pieced together the story of a remarkable man.

No one remembers what became of his parents, only that he was brought up by Sir Frank Brangwyn, a Welsh artist. By the 1920s Brangwyn was fêted. He was the first living artist to be given a one-man exhibition by the Royal Academy. It was opened by the Prime Minister. A critic extolled the 'juicy quality' in his work that 'Mr Whistler reproduces so well'. D. H. Lawrence, a keen amateur, said, 'To copy a Frank Brangwyn is a joy, so refreshing.' He became even more famous for his huge murals such as those that decorate the walls of the Royal Exchange in London and the Rockefeller Center in New York.

Cam trained as a physiologist, and went to work at the Royal Naval Physiological Laboratory at Alverstoke in Hampshire. In those days it was an array of ramshackle wooden huts that had started life as cargo containers; they were devoid of heating and ventilated by stable doors. An inspecting parliamentary committee concluded that the conditions in which the experimental goats were kept, though far from satisfactory, were at least better than those endured by the scientists.

In the early days, when Cam was affectionately known as Camiknickers, he carried out risky experiments on the effects of X-rays on human tissue – *his* human tissue. With the outbreak of war, new challenges arose. Sir Henry Tizard, scientific adviser to the Ministry of Aircraft Production, asked Wright if he would help out on 'something frightfully hush-hush'. Barnes Wallis had designed a bomb that in theory could skip across water to explode at the base of a dam. Wright was to be the on-board observer during the trials.

A Wellington bomber had been specially modified for the task. With its bomb doors removed and a sphere protruding beneath, the aircraft's outline once puzzled naval gunners who opened fire in case it was an enemy plane. The trials were dogged with near-disasters. One bomb fragmented and shrapnel perforated the aeroplane's elevators; another produced such a water spout when dropped that it damaged the wings. On both occasions the plane just managed to land safely.

After many failures the bomb was trained to bounce. But could it blow a hole in a dam? 'There's a small disused dam in

Radnorshire,' said Wallis. 'No earthly use any more . . . and won't ever be missed. We could try and knock it down.'

So Wright found himself flying over Wales. He started the motor that set the bomb whirling on a spindle; it was top spin that enabled the round bomb to skip across the water. But the mechanism didn't release the bomb. It spun faster and faster and smoke poured from the spindle. The bomb was primed to explode and time was ticking away. Wright grabbed an overhead strut and suspended himself behind the bomb bay, swung his legs into the air and kicked at the bomb. Time after time his feet shot off the spinning sphere and he lurched forward over the bomb. He later admitted to thinking, 'This is not only dangerous, but a bloody absurd way to get killed.' Suddenly the bomb fell free and left Cam dangling over the open bay whilst the dam exploded beneath him.

Another project involved a device designed to blow gaps in shore defences during the D-Day landings. Attached to the prow of a boat was a rocket launcher. The idea was that the rocket would zoom up the beach dragging a long tail of fire-hose which would rip a path through tangles of barbed wire. It was Wright's job to test it. The landing craft nosed on to the beach and the rocket shot away at a ferocious velocity. The hose uncoiled as planned but, as its other end was fixed to the craft, it wrenched off the entire front deck of the boat, which flew up the beach like a demented kite. 'I just shut my eyes,' Cam confessed, 'and hoped to hell there was nobody sunbathing on the other side of the dunes.'

When the war ended, the atmosphere at the Alverstoke laboratory became more relaxed, almost soporific. The experimental goats munched lazily on the lawn. Most of the personnel lounged about and, when in need of exercise, played chess. The director would amble about suggesting that perhaps the queen was vulnerable as the bishop had exposed himself. When Cam expressed impatience at the regime, he was told not to fret, and to learn to play chess.

This did not suit him at all. He was tall, nimble and wiry, an active, restless man, who wanted to get on with the job, solve the problem and move on to the next task. He spoke 'rapidly and incisively with frequent and often abrupt changes of topic'. Although practical problems fascinated him, he had no interest in airy-fairy philosophy or abstract ideas, or chess.

He was a natural leader, swift to praise and to make decisions. But even those who admired him took care not to tread on his sensitivities. He did not like to be wrong or be seen to make mistakes, although he was understanding of the errors of others and furious in the defence of his friends. But, if he wanted to be treated with respect, he had come to the wrong place.

Life was rarely tranquil in the laboratory. None of the teams collaborated. Some of the staff were not on speaking terms and communicated only via a chain of intermediaries. Relations with the laboratory director, who had been promoted over Wright's head, became so bad that they would often steam out to collide in mid-lawn and have a set-to in front of the entire lab, then, puffing and puce, they would return to their rooms as if nothing had happened. When Cam was recommended for an award the director tried, but failed, to block it and subsequently had to make a public acknowledgement of his achievements.

Explosions of all kinds were Cam's speciality. One of his delights was to show newcomers around the establishment and introduce them to some of the research. He once ushered a group around a circular steel tank full of water. There was little to be seen in it. It didn't contain any experimental animals. At least, not yet.

'I shall now demonstrate the effects of an underwater explosion,' he announced ominously. 'Roll up the right-hand shirt sleeve and stick your arm in the water.' They did so with muted enthusiasm. 'Right. Fire!'

There was a loud retort and a plume of water rose from the centre of the tank. The victims assumed that their arms had been amputated at the elbow.

'That,' said Wright cheerfully, 'is what a mere 1.5 grams of explosives feels like. Now put the other arm into one of these tubes and then immerse it in the tank.'

Reluctantly they slipped on a variety of metal drainpipes and foam-rubber sleeves.

'Fire!'

Those wearing drainpipes now had two arms that felt as if they had been blown off, whereas the rubber-clad victims suffered hardly at all. 'There you are,' said Wright, 'a pressure of 1,000 pounds per square inch and there are no harmful effects if you wear rubber. Just to prove there is no trick involved, those wearing rubber sleeves, please exchange them for drainpipes and we will complete the demonstration.'

Wright, by experience, became an authority on underwater injuries. Explosions are dangerous under water because, although shrapnel doesn't fly very far, the incompressibility of water allows the shock wave to travel much further than in air. He had earlier developed suits designed to protect underwater saboteurs from blast. They were tested by tossing explosives into the water to see how the diver got on. Although he paid volunteers as much as two shillings and sixpence (12p) a day, Wright himself was invariably a guinea-pig.

Wright became secretary of the Underwater Blast Committee. Their remit was to predict the effects of depth charges on survivors of sunken ships or submarines. With a physicist, A. H. Bebb, he examined the dual deadly effects of underwater explosions, the shock wave that can shatter the diver and the 'water ram' effect that follows behind to crush him. Cam interviewed many survivors of explosions at sea and repeatedly heard stories of how their companions had suddenly lost the power to move their arms and legs, given out a little gasp, then slowly disappeared beneath the waves. He also attended many post mortems on servicemen killed in explosions so that he could equate their injuries to those induced experimentally on animals by blasts of known size. He compiled a reference file of photographs of the awful injuries inflicted by explosions. Yet often gross internal injuries gave no external sign.

To test the possible insulating effects of an air cushion Wright relaxed on a floating air bed whilst an enormous explosion was set off beneath him. He is said to have flown a good distance, but to have landed unharmed. Much of the research involved suspending volunteer navy divers, plus Wright, at different depths in the sea and setting off progressively larger explosive charges of TNT at ever-decreasing distances from the 'victim'. 'It was like being hit over the head with a cricket bat,' a diver confided. After suffering about thirty blasts each, their symptoms were wheezy chests and harsh breathing and even broken ribs, as well as ruptured ear drums. As a result, it was decided not to expose naval divers to further blasts at this depth.

Wright was puzzled that large, distant explosions sometimes did more damage than smaller explosions closer to, which in theory were more dangerous. So he dived to 50 feet and a 200lb charge was detonated just over 2000 feet away. The shattering effect of the blast wave left Wright with severe pain in his back, unable to move his arms and legs and losing consciousness.

He was hauled out paralysed and bleeding profusely from his mouth, nose and ears.

Whilst slowly recovering in hospital, Wright mused on the cause of his injuries. He had previously withstood closer, smaller blasts that were calculated to give a maximum shock-wave pressure ten times greater than that which had disabled him at long range. He concluded that because he was suspended in mid-water he wasn't struck just once by the blast, but several times almost simultaneously. In relatively shallow water with a rocky sea floor, the shock waves not only travelled directly through the water, but were also reflected from the sea bottom to the surface and from surface to bottom. By ill-luck he had been suspended in mid-water at a place where these sets of shock waves met. When he recovered, he resumed his experiments and again subjected himself to the same experimental explosion, but at a depth at which he calculated he would miss the multiple blast. Thankfully he did.

A few years later he was scheduled to lecture on the effects of underwater blasts, but was called away and a colleague stepped in. One exhibit was the chest X-ray of some poor fellow whose lungs had been half shredded by an explosion. The curious colleague peeled back a label in the corner to reveal the patient's name. It was, of course, Cameron Wright.

Another task was to help airmen to escape from ditched aircraft that were sinking. The quandary was whether they should fire the ejector seat. Water is much denser than air so that when the charge of cordite exploded it might not eject the pilot and his seat, but ram the seat through the pilot. Added to this was the fear that accelerating rapidly through water with explosives up his behind might dislodge the pilot's goggles and tear off his arms and legs. The Admiralty sent navy surgeon John Rawlins to consult with Wright. Cam estimated the drag and G-forces and advised against ejecting, but, by chance, only twenty-four hours later an over-enthusiastic deck crew maoeuvred a fighter over the side of an aircraft carrier into the water. The drowning pilot fired his ejector seat and was rescued alive. So Rawlins started a six-year research programme to determine how the pilot survived and to develop a successful underwater escape system. Wright's contributions included a device for determining the water level in the cockpit and an underwater communication system.

He was an inveterate inventor and produced hot water from a cold-water tap by fitting an induction coil around the faucet. It was a precursor of the microwave cooker, but he was not allowed to develop it as it was considered too dangerous.

Not all his gadgets were successful. The president of the Royal College of Surgeons one day complained to him that members often forgot to flush the lavatory. So Wright designed and installed an automatically flushing loo. It was a mechanical system that triggered the valve when the occupant rose from the seat. Cam tested it and it worked like magic. Unfortunately, on its very first night of operation, an ancient retired surgeon allowed his shirt tail to dangle into the mechanism and when he tried to rise, he couldn't. Eventually, his cries were heard and the door was broken down to reveal a tiny bearded man in a top hat with his trousers around his ankles.

Wright was responsible for all the animals kept at the Laboratory. Goats and sheep were used as surrogates for men in experiments. The operating theatre was well equipped and Wright had supervised its refurbishment. Colleagues remember him sheathed in a green theatre gown, 'gloved hands entwined, elbows flexed, body tilted slightly forward, peeping over his half-spectacles, making last-minute adjustments and checking every minute detail to ensure that the animals . . . were accorded the same rigorous and humane attention as would their human counterparts.' He examined animals to look for any internal symptoms following exposure to blast or pressure changes. One unexpected result showed that increased pressure around damaged bone induced the growth of new bone tissue.

Cam took the term operating *theatre* literally. One one occasion, when a young assistant was inserting a tube down the throat of an anaesthetised sheep, Cam, to amuse visitors, playfully lifted up the tail, peered in and shouted, 'Stop! Too far!'

Wright had no medical qualifications and longed for a degree in surgery. Later, arrangements were made for him to do a course on experimental surgery at the Mayo Clinic, but by then his failing eyesight prevented it. Even so, this did not inhibit him from pioneering advances in anaesthesiology, plastic surgery, bone grafting and surgical pathology.

He was, however, wary of relying solely on data from animals for they were unable to tell you how they felt. He much preferred to experiment on people, and never asked a colleague to do anything he wouldn't risk himself. This was small comfort to them as he was fearless. In 1965 he cut out a tumour from the back of his hand unassisted.

Shortly after the end of the Second World War it was discovered that almost all the submariners escaping from damaged submarines had done so without using the escape hatches or the regulation breathing apparatus provided. The escapees took a deep breath then came up through holes in the damaged hull, breathing out all the way so that the decreasing pressure did not rupture their lungs. The Admiralty wanted to know whether this could be done safely from great depth. But attempting such a thing from hundreds of feet down was a frightening prospect.

Would a lungful of air last that long? Would there be sufficient oxygen in the lungs at depth to prevent the escapee from suffocating on the way up?

The Laboratory Superintendent decided that the required experiments were far too dangerous, but, when he was on holiday, Cam did them anyway. He lay submerged in cold water in a laboratory chamber pressurised to the equivalent of 300 feet depth and then exhaled whilst the pressure was rapidly reduced. He discovered that even to close the mouth for a moment risked making one's lungs inflate and burst. The experiment was described by a colleague as 'a typical example of corner cutting, but a very brave and remarkable thing to do'. As a result of his experiments the Royal Navy adopted the technique of free, buoyant ascent from depths as great as 600 feet and HMS *Dolphin*, a land-based training establishment, built a tank 100 feet deep in which submariners could practise ascents.

In 1950 Wright was awarded the OBE 'for courage in simulating a free ascent from a submarine at 300 feet and facing the underwater blast of a 200 lb charge at a range of 2,000 feet off Spithead'.

Cam was ever ready to help and advise fellow researchers. 'Ask him a trivial question and he would come back weeks later with reference, equations and the answer in his inimitable handwriting. Give him a trifling manuscript to read and he would annotate it as carefully and conscientiously as if you were the Director General himself.' Once, a young colleague who was using ultrasound to detect the onset of decompression sickness couldn't find a suitable place on the human body to attach the transducer. He outlined the problem to Wright. The tissue had to be well vasculated and he had tried almost everywhere. 'Scrotum!' Cam declared, knowing that was not a place he would have dared to test on burly Royal Engineer divers. After a few personal trials, the researcher was relieved to find that the scrotum was no better than the ear lobe.

Wright was lean but immensely strong. When a new member of staff was being interviewed, he strode into the room and introduced himself. On discovering the interviewee was Welsh, he said, 'Then you must be a rugby player', thrust his hands into the candidate's armpits and lifted him clear of the ground to test his weight. When working with navy divers he stayed at the Albion Hotel in Falmouth. They wanted to use the dance hall for a party, but the grand piano was in a room some distance away. The divers asked at the reception desk if they might move it, but on returning to the dance hall they were astounded to see it gliding into the room of its own volition. Wright was crouching beneath, carrying it on his back. He was the divers' hero from that day forward. Another time when he was out with the divers he saw some goats in a paddock and vaulted the fence to join them. Down on all fours he playfully butted a young billy who retreated, then charged – and knocked Cam out cold.

Wright advised on the development of experimental surgery at the Royal Veterinary College and thereafter, although not a qualified vet, was permitted to carry out animal work outside the Physiological Laboratory. One of his friends had a farm and wanted to sell a prize bull for stud. Unfortunately, it had only one testicle. Although this in no way impaired its fertility, it might well put off potential buyers. 'That's no problem,' Wright declared, 'I'll make him one.' A bull's ball was duly modelled from dental wax. Wright's creation was a perfect match, at least until the bull slept on it, melted the wax and ended up with a testicle accompanied by a gramophone record.

To the envy of his colleagues Cam had a succession of pretty

female assistants, some of whom he took for a spin in his Alpha-
Romeo convertible. One he invited out for a picnic followed by
horse riding. He was an excellent rider who loved horses and
spent his holidays in Ireland riding with the Kildare Hunt. She,
on the other hand, was a little nervous as she hadn't been in the
saddle for years and feared getting a sore rump. 'Tell you what,'
said Cam, 'I'll take some tape which you can stick across the lower
inner side of your cheeks and that'll stop any chafing. Works a
treat. I've saddle-tested it myself.' She was convinced and, after
the picnic, retired to a pub lavatory taking the picnic basket in
which Cam had placed a large roll of four-inch-wide adhesive
tape. She failed to return for over half an hour and then hobbled
towards the car in tears and with a large lump in her jodhpurs.

'What on earth's the matter?' Cam enquired.

'Your bloody Elastoplast is the matter. I can't get it off.'

As she had been applying the adhesive tape the roll had
sprung from her hand and stuck to her pubic hair. Unfortunately,
Cam had forgotten to pack the scissors and, as she couldn't pull
it off, she had to return with the entire roll stuck down her
trousers.

'Please help me,' she sobbed.

So they drove to a quiet lane and he carefully cut away her
pubic hair with a bread knife until eventually the tape came away.
Wright confessed that 'No experience I have ever had either
under water or on the surface was quite so traumatic.' She never
spoke to him again.

His car was his pride and joy. He had rebuilt it from the
chassis with parts cannibalised from two other Alpha-Romeos
that he had in the garage. It became a work of art, a cascade of
chrome against gleaming paint, and won prizes at *concours d'élégance*.
Every part was stamped and dated; 'even the screws were tabu-

lated'. His driving style was to accelerate fiercely and go as fast as the law would allow – and then a little bit faster.

Wright retired alone to Winchester with his favourite recordings of Kathleen Ferrier and Sir John Barbirolli. But he was too energetic to be idle. An appointment as Consultant Experimental Surgeon at the Eastman Dental Clinic in London and collaboration with surgeons at Southampton gave him the scope to devise instruments for localising fibre tracts in the spinal chord, and to develop the use of ultrasound for non-invasive surgery.

He changed little; the eyebrows were whiter now and a little bushier, but he still wore his outdoor uniform of tweed hat, jacket and baggy trousers, but never an overcoat, whatever the weather. When old colleagues dropped in, he would regale them with tales of his adventures or show them portfolios of drawings by his artist guardian, Sir Frank Brangwyn. As often as not he would let them choose one to keep.

He was in hospital when the lungs he had shattered years before finally let him down. Even when he came to know the full meaning of illness, he faced it with his usual courage. The window in his ward overlooked the Solent, close to the scene of his most dangerous exploits.

Everyone remembers Cameron Wright as brave, talented and entertaining. Yet he remained a mystery even to his friends. Although always ready to give a sympathetic ear to others, he rarely spoke of his own personal life. He had 'an outstanding and indubitable gift for friendship', but his standards were exacting. He hated pretension or hypocrisy and valued courage, loyalty and integrity, and assumed these qualities in others. Should they fall short of his expectations, he could not overlook it; he was implacable in his condemnation of those who broke the code.

He was a paradox, a sociable loner, forthright and obstinate yet shy, a bachelor to the bone who was seldom without the company of women, a rebel who loved to prove other experts wrong, but expected their admiration.

From the moment you met him you knew you were in the presence of a 'lovable and remarkable man', someone who had not wasted a moment of his life doing anything but living.

Submariner making a free ascent (*Drawing by Win Norton*)

SHOTS IN THE DARK

When we leaf through the family album we often wonder at how blurred we were in our youth. Yet these snaps were taken in summer sunshine beside the sea, not beneath it.

Those who have never tried to film below the waves can have little feeling for the difficulties of working in salt water keen on corrosion and seeping into every seal, taking any watertight container as a challenge. Water also steals the light as you descend and purloins colours one at a time, the red rays first. At depth you bleed black smoke.

Worst of all, someone has scattered plankton and silt in front of the lens so that the flash, should it work, picks out every speck. You might as well take photographs in lentil soup.

But at least today's diver has the benefit of excellent equipment perfected over the years. How different it was for the pioneers who often had to improvise their gear and had no one to turn to for advice. They were shooting in the dark.

Louis Boutan dressed for the shore at Banyuls sur Mer, around 1890
(*From the archives of Steven Weinberg*)

A cultured pearl

Louis Marie-Auguste Boutan 1859–1934

Louis Boutan was born in Versailles into a family that prized education. His father was a physics teacher and expected Louis to do well at school. Luckily, he did. But beneath the swot with bright brown eyes lurked an adventurer longing for mountains to climb.

As an adolescent he was thrilled by the alpine adventures of some family friends. Determined to rise to new heights, young Louis set off to scale a glacier. Alone in the ice fields of the Pyrenees, however, he suffered from both forms of cold feet, retreated to the nearest town and spent his last few sous on tobacco. In search of a miracle he then trudged to Lourdes, where a relative returned him to his family.

At twenty he was appointed as a demonstrator, the lowliest academic position at the University of Paris, but was hardly seated at the laboratory bench when the Minister of Public Instruction despatched him on an expedition to Australia to coincide with the Melbourne Exposition.

He sailed on the warship *Finistère* and spent eighteen months exploring Victoria and New South Wales, crossing the Murray Plains, and scaling the eucalyptus-scented Blue Mountains west of Sydney. These were wild colonial days in the outback. He rode with a pistol at his hip and a rifle over his shoulder and sometimes they were needed. He hunted kangaroo at the gallop and fought off sheep rustlers. In the evening he camped with squatters and colonists who, to Louis' astonishment, for dinner shed their dust-bitten clothes and donned smoking-jackets.

He visited the gold mines north of Melbourne and met up with an old Gallic prospector who was so delighted to converse in French again that he implored Louis to stay. Fifty years later a wistful Louis regretted having declined. He would have loved to have sieved the rivers and burrowed into the hills in search of something glistening in the darkness. Instead, he sought nuggets of knowledge from his research.

At the time he was pledged to capture specimens of the soon to be extinct Tasmanian wolves, kangaroo rats, Australian 'squirrels' for the Paris zoo, and marsupial foetuses for the Muséum. He also collected seeds from the salt bushes of the plains which during the dry season were the sole browse of the sheep. The idea was that they might be introduced into the arid areas of Algeria as summer fodder. It was the great age of bringing back potentially useful plants from the tropics and inducing them to grow in Europe or her nearby colonies. Most of Europe's botanical gardens were originally 'Gardens of Acclimatisation'. Unfortunately the salt bushes stubbornly insisted on flowering at the appropriate season for Australia and failed to seed themselves in Algeria.

Boutan noticed that the Australian vines were being attacked by a root louse. He immediately produced a report for the state government on how the pest had been combated in Europe and lectured widely on how native vines might be grafted on to resistant American root stocks.

On his journey home through the Torres Strait, he recalled

the chapter in Jules Verne's *Twenty Thousand Leagues Under the Sea* in which the submarine *Nautilus* went aground in these waters and Professor Aronnax had gathered sea cucumbers and oysters. Boutan plunged down naked with native pearl-divers and saw for the first time the richness of tropical marine life, the vibrant flickering fish, the pulsing ghosts of medusae. It was a revelation for someone trained on preserved specimens, stiff and leached of colour. He also saw the silky pearls that grew inside the oysters, and an idea began to grow inside him.

Back in Paris, his professor encouraged Boutan's marine studies, but he was a famous tyrant who made life uncomfortable for his protégés. Boutan never criticised the professor, but when he found a new species of lizard in a cave where little light penetrated, he named the beast after him.

Louis' teaching duties burgeoned and his spirit shrivelled in the hushed respectability of the museum where the silence was broken only by the scratching of nibs and the occasional clink of pickling jars. If he were to do any *real* research he must get away. Whenever he could he decamped to the marine laboratories at Banyuls-sur-Mer on the Mediterranean or Roscoff on the Atlantic coast. He studied keyhole limpets and hired a local fishing boat to go dredging for urchins and scallops. In the wind and the watery sunlight he dreamed of the tropics.

In 1891 he persuaded a sponsor to fund an expedition. He set up a small laboratory in Suez on the banks of the misnamed Sweet Water Canal. In the Suez Canal, which had only been open for 22 years, he found a species of mollusc that he had first seen in Australia, and that was now spreading northwards. So many species would eventually pass through the Canal from the rich Indian Ocean into the impoverished Mediterranean, that the phenomenon would be called 'Lessepsian migration' after de

Lesseps, the builder of the Canal.

In a local fishing boat Boutan zigzagged across the Red Sea, spending half the time tossed by storms, the rest becalmed. When the wind got up, the boat had a tendency 'to rock in an alarming fashion'. Although the crew were skilled at casting a weighted net to ensnare the sliding, silver fish, their knowledge of navigation was limited – they could not even recognise the Pole Star. Thus all the voyages were made during the heat of day. At dusk they anchored, often miles out to sea far from the jagged coastal reefs.

On a rare expedition ashore, Boutan, with rifle at the ready, trudged for four and a half hours across wind-sifted dunes towards Mount Hammân Fara'ûn on which drifts of pure white sand gave the unreal illusion of snow on the baking rock. Nearby he explored thermal pools in hot underground caves and returned to the boat exhausted.

Before he left this coast Louis dragged the sea floor for snails and fish, but often the dredge snagged on a reef and almost over-turned the boat. The crew swapped tobacco for local produce and set off back towards Suez with the boat strewn with dead fish that exuded a 'strong and scarcely fragrant odour'.

Boutan spent his last few days at Tûr where, in the shelter of the reef, he found the richest collecting ground of the trip. He wanted to stay longer, but it was right beside the Campement Sanitaire where pilgrims with cholera were quarantined, and the cholera season was imminent . . .

Boutan's thirst for adventure had not yet been quenched and France still had unexplored colonies aplenty. In 1904 he organised a trip to Madagascar, but on the eve of departure the funds vanished with a change of government. Before he had time to nurture his disappointment, the Academy of Science invited him to lead a scientific expedition to Indo-China. For four years Louis explored the shores and jungles of Vietnam, Laos and Cambodia. He trekked thousands of miles, crossed mountains, traced rivers, including the mighty Mekong, and followed a route that would one day become the infamous Ho Chi Minh trail.

On his journeys he inventoried the fauna and flora and studied everything from the parasites of coffee plants to the habits of bears and monkeys. He even found time to write his classic *Décades Zoologiques*, which was beautifully illustrated by local artists.

The mission was abruptly terminated and Louis returned to France with his notes and memories and a young gibbon christened Pépée which he kept for many years to study communication in apes.

His reputation as a naturalist was growing, yet one of his

Boutan bursting for air in the 1890s

most outstanding achievements was at that time considered a side-show of little interest to scientists. Boutan's first love had always been the ocean. His students called him the 'Sea Wolf', for he rarely missed an opportunity to go out with them on the boat or follow down a tide to see what mysteries were uncovered. He was 'an enthusiastic dredger' and aware that for every species he met on the shore there were five or six lurking below the waves, if only he could get at them.

He compared the land-bound marine biologist to the alien visitor from the moon observing us from his spaceship floating on top of the atmosphere: 'If this lunatic wished to do research on the inhabitants of the globe . . . he would drag and net, and perhaps dive down the anchor rope of his balloon.'

Around 1890 he used the traditional hard-hat diving dress for the first time to venture beneath the sea: 'The strangeness of the undersea landscape made a very vivid impression on me and it seemed unfortunate that I could not translate this into a more or less exact description . . . I would like to be able to bring back from these explorations a more tangible souvenir; but it is scarcely possible, even a good diver cannot make a good picture or even a sketch of the depths. I resolved to make a photographic image!'

Although Boutan did not know it, such an image already existed. In 1856 William Thompson, an English gentleman naturalist, had sealed his camera inside a box fitted with a glass window and lowered it eighteen feet down into the sea. Both the box and the camera flooded, but after a ten-minute exposure there was an image on the plate. It was not brilliant, there is even some dispute as to which way up the picture should be viewed, but it was the first underwater photograph. 'This application of photography may prove of incalculable benefit to science,' Thompson predicted, but it was his only attempt. No one followed in his prints until Louis Boutan, thirty-six years later.

Boutan's first photographs were taken in 1892 with a camera using large glass plates and enclosed in a watertight metal box that he had designed. It had a rubber bladder on the outside which, when squeezed by water, pushed air into the box to counteract the increasing pressure. This is how he described his first attempts:

> 'I first sought to explore the Bay of Banyuls with my lens . . . Subjects for photography, however, are numerous and varied . . . But when you go down in a diving suit, the silt . . . constitutes a serious obstacle to obtaining good undersea shots . . . the contrasts are not sufficient to give sharp blacks and whites and the pictures obtained are necessarily dull . . . At each step the diver raises a cloud of mud which stays in suspension for several minutes and darkens the water through which the light rays must pass. I persisted, however . . . until I obtained a series of pictures which, if not all that good, were at least adequate.
>
> I decided to look for a more favourable spot . . . I found it a little south of the laboratory in a small cove briskly washed by the swell . . . The bottom is carpeted with undersea meadows which dip in a gentle slope towards the high seas. Violent currents . . . have brought about the formation of sandy patches that criss-cross the meadows . . . Nothing is more impressive than to follow one of these roads; on each side . . . stretch tall

stems of Posidonia [sea grass] whose luxuriant growth and aspect recall the plants of a tropical country. The diver finds himself surrounded by a green wall, for the stems of these singular plants reach as high as his helmet . . .

Here is the procedure that I adopted to get my pictures . . . After having landed at the desired depth, I signalled the captain to lower the different parts of the photographic equipment. On the end of a line I received the iron platform, the camera in its case, and a weight to anchor everything.

The view chosen, I would set up the base of the apparatus at leisure and arrange the camera in such a way as to have only to press a button to open the shutter. This done, I sent another signal to the captain who held the life-line in his hand. This signal indicated that the exposure had begun, and I would wait patiently for the captain to indicate the end of the operation. You understand, of course, that it is impossible . . . to take a watch down in a diving suit to time the exposure. Thanks to the method that I had adopted, this difficulty was overcome; the captain's job was to consult his watch and warn me in time.

His main problem was that the film emulsion was so slow that the plates had to be exposed for half an hour or more if he stopped down to increase the sharpness. Long exposures are use-

less under water where, even on a calm day, the seagrass sways to
and fro and detached weed languidly drifts past in front of the lens.

The pictures were blurred, but Boutan was not dismayed. 'Is
water an unsuitable medium for getting good photographs? The
experience of these last three years has proved to me that the
medium of water was in no way guilty and that if the camera were
improved, much better pictures would result.'

Another problem with the clumsy plate camera was that the
waterproof case had to be opened on the surface after each exposure, in order to change plates. Fortunately, manufacturers had
begun to produce much more compact cameras popularly known
as 'Detectives' because they could be hidden within one's clothes
to take surreptitious snaps. They were also able to take several
shots without reloading and the lens allowed everything beyond
three or four metres to be in focus. They were just what Boutan
needed and soon he was taking 'instantaneous' exposures of ten
seconds. At last recognisable images were captured on film.

For photography in the shallows, he waded in, chest deep,
with a camera fixed inside a glass-bottomed viewing box.
Amazingly he also tried using a flooded camera and, although the
wash wave of the shutter blurred the image, he claimed neither the
film emulsion (specially prepared for him by the Lumière
brothers) nor the camera was damaged.

For photographs in deeper water Boutan would first have to
pierce the gloom with artificial light. His prototype illuminator
was a glass bell jar full of oxygen through which passed a coiled
filament of magnesium wire. Electrical current from a battery
caused the filament to glow brightly, but the combustion was
unpredictable and the jar soon became clouded with magnesium
dust. He abandoned the method reluctantly. 'I believe I may have
rejected it too soon. With a few modifications, it might be

improved.' Indeed it might; it was the progenitor of the modern flash bulb.

An improved model worked on an entirely different principle. In this, the bell jar contained a lighted alcohol lamp and squeezing a rubber bulb fired magnesium powder into the flame producing a spectacular flash of light. The reservoir of powder was sufficient for several firings. Louis had invented the most sophisticated flash gun up to that time and, what is more, it worked under water.

He wanted to make much more powerful watertight lights, but the cost was prohibitive. Then the president of a major optical manufacturing company came through his door asking for underwater photographs for the Paris Exposition. He funded and built two electric arc lamps with which Louis, using a remotely operated camera with an electro-magnetic shutter, took photographs at the amazing depth of 165 feet.

Cartoons of a loony professor taking underwater snaps of the legs of bathing belles appeared in the newspapers. Louis smiled and retaliated with an underwater shot of the lower reaches of three friends in their striped woollen bathing costumes.

In 1900 he published the first-ever manual of underwater photography. His aims were modest: 'I have just tried to give a detailed account of my work on underwater photography and thus draw the attention of workers to an application that will render great service to undersea research . . . My aims will be fully achieved if a few readers are sufficiently interested to take undersea pictures themselves.'

He need not have doubted it. Within fourteen years John Williamson was making underwater movies and in 1923 an American diving biologist, W. H. Longley, took the first underwater shots in colour. He used slow film whose colour was derived from millions of embedded grains of tinted starch. To provide the light needed, he exploded one-pound charges of powdered magnesium on an opened-bottomed raft floating above. The blast was equivalent to 2,400 flash bulbs and was the brightest light ever used for underwater shots. It was almost 'more than human nerves could stand', certainly more than the raft could stand, for one explosion blew it to smithereens.

Boutan had started something, but now he returned to his marine biology, studying how mussels make the 'guy ropes' that tether them to the rock. The shellfish gracefully extended its muscular 'foot', folding it to form a groove, just as you roll your tongue. An adhesive that sets immediately on contact with water was secreted down the groove, then the 'foot' was withdrawn, leaving the thread fixed to the rock. All over the Mediterranean, the silky attachment threads of the giant *Pinna* clam were once woven into fine robes, and Jules Verne kitted out the crew of the *Nautilus* in suits of *Pinna* fibres.

Boutan also followed up Milne Edwards' studies on the development of molluscs from their minute larvae. His trial animal was the ormer, a small abalone which has a beautiful blue nacre inside the shell. Lining the shell is a thin membrane called the mantle and, Boutan argued, as it is the only tissue in contact with the shell it must secrete the nacre. He carefully detached part of the shell and managed to keep the animal alive long enough to show that the mantle did indeed produce a replacement shell and was also responsible for its lustrous lining.

Louis had admired the pearls in shells he had seen in Australia. Did the mantle produce these too? Perhaps it would secrete mother-of-pearl over any object with which it came into contact. Boutan devised an ingenious test of this idea. He trepanned an ormer by drilling a small hole through the shell, taking care not to damage the delicate mantle beneath. He inserted a tiny fragment of nacre into the hole and tucked it down between the mantle and the shell. Within a few months this 'seed' became a smooth hemisphere of mother-of-pearl. Clearly, natural pearls were produced when a sand grain irritated the mantle and was neutralised by being coated with nacre. Boutan concluded that any shell with a nacreous lining could potentially produce pearls and went on to prove it experimentally.

He tried to persuade the Governor General of Indo-China that the large mussels he had seen there would be ideal for the production of cultured pearls and that it could become a commercial industry, but nothing happened. Boutan's preliminary findings were published in the scientific literature in 1898. There followed a series of seventeen papers in which he demonstrated how perfect, round pearls could be induced.

A Japanese noodle salesman who had tried to grow pearls was the only one to spot the potential of these discoveries, and in 1920 commercial quantities of his cultured pearls appeared in Paris. They were almost indistinguishable from the 'real' thing. There was panic within the pearl cartel that fixed world prices, for the value of their stocks of natural pearls would plummet. They claimed that the market was being flooded with 'fraudulent' pearls. The importer was arrested and sent for trial. Boutan was the star witness. The cultured pearl, he testified, was as natural as the 'wild' one. The oyster cared little whether the pearl was induced by nature or by man. The trial made Boutan a celebrity, but put paid to the Parisian fashion for pearls.

There was soon a major pearl-culturing industry in the orient. A great opportunity had been lost to France, but Boutan's great review, *La Perle*, does not contain a single word of recrimination.

I imagine that Boutan would have been delighted that current research on nacre has shown that although it is 95 per cent
chalk, its structure (tiny plates woven together with a silk-like
protein) converts it into a ceramic several thousand times stronger
than chalk. It is now being manufactured (using exactly the same
technology as for puff pastry) for use as turbine blades in jet
engines where uncooled metal blades would melt.

During The Great War, Louis and his brother, Auguste, an
engineer and director of the Lyon Gas Company, turned their
energies to inventing a self-contained underwater breathing apparatus. It used a cylinder of compressed air charged to a pressure
of almost 200 atmospheres, the same as a modern diver's air tank.
Although the gear was tricky to use, it was adopted as standard on
French submarines. The idea was that it would allow a diver to
leave the vessel under water and perhaps make minor repairs or
free the hull from an entangling net. They also designed an underwater 'chariot', a manned torpedo similar to those used for sab-
otage during the Second World War. Both Boutan brothers were
awarded the Légion d'Honneur 'for service to national defence'.

From 1919 Louis was Professor of Zoology and Animal
Physiology at the University of Bordeaux, but as he gazed from
his office window he longed once more for the sea and the shore.
The nearest coast to Bordeaux was, for a marine biologist, the
dullest in France. He read Milne Edwards' vivid account of
Algerian shores, and a chance meeting at a conference with a
professor from Algeria led to a job swap. So, in 1924 Louis found
himself not only Professor of Zoology in Algiers, but also the
director of a station for experimental aquaculture and Government Inspector of Fisheries.

From the day he stepped ashore in Africa he knew he would
never leave. He was in his element and, as often as not, on his

element, the sea. He sailed with fishermen and promoted new fisheries for shrimps, and even sharks, for it was possible to utilise their meat, their oil, their skins as 'leather', and at the same time 'purge the sea of undesirable predators'. He wrote papers evaluating the merits of fishing with rifles and explosives. At the aquaculture station he developed ways of culturing oysters, clams and shrimps and the means to despatch them alive to France.

Best of all, he went out on the research boat with his students. He seems to have nurtured an easy camaraderie with his protégés in an age when it was more usual for disciples to sit respectfully at the master's feet waiting to agree with him. On calm nights with the distant shore lights merging with the stars, they would sit on deck smoking their pipes. 'This is the *real* life,' he assured them.

Honours accumulated and in 1929 he retired with his mistress to a coastal villa called Djouara (Arabic for 'Pearl'). The walls were painted with sea creatures and monsters of the deep. He cultivated roses and read the classics, sketched a little and wrote novels, poems and plays. They lived quietly, then quietly one night he died. From the little cemetery where he is buried you can hear the waves chafing the shore on which he loved to walk.

He was admired and much loved, a gregarious man who nonetheless worked best alone, away from the conflict that arose in groups. 'The man was goodness itself,' a friend declared, 'with a generous heart.' He never gave a second thought to the fortune he had forfeited by not patenting his methods for culturing pearls, and he had even saved the day for those who had exploited his invention. A generous heart indeed.

Louis Boutan considered science 'the quest for beauty'. He epitomised the versatile scientist/naturalist. What contemporary biologist, having invented underwater photography and the cultured pearl and saved the Australian wine industry, would have had the knowledge and energy to write authoritatively on the beaks of birds, the language of apes and the untwisting of snails?

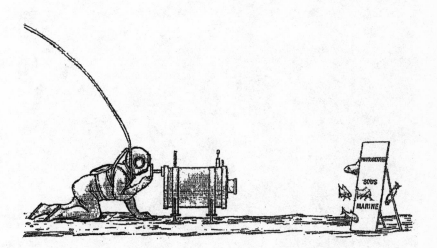

Boutan in 'Hard hat' suit creeping up on a subject to photograph

John Williamson climbing down into the submarine tube carrying his baby
daughter, Sylvia, wearing a sailor's cap
(*All photographs by permission of Sylvia Munro*)

The man with the amazing tube

John Ernest Williamson 1881–1966

On the day Ernest Williamson was born his father was rounding Cape Horn, and he was almost three when he saw him for the first time. 'I remember hazily the day he breezed into our home at Liverpool, bringing with him the tang of the sea.' The sea was in his father's blood and now it lodged in Ernest's imagination.

'I don't think he more than glanced at me for he carried in with him his latest invention . . . he had brought home a baby of his own.' It was a collapsible pram.

His Scottish father was a ship's captain by trade, but an inventor by inclination. Each time he returned from a voyage he brought a new device he had been working on. One idea had come to him whilst observing fishing boats bobbing in the swell off Newfoundland, their port and starboard lights visible even though the vessels themselves were lost in fog. The winking red and green lights gave him the basis for a signalling system. It looked like a winner and he placed the plans in the hands of an agent in New York who would bring the device to the market. Months later, when his ship took him back to New York, he found the agent had fled and that his device had been patented under another name. America was the land of opportunity and the agent had seized his.

His father was incensed and immediately left the navy to pursue the missing agent. First he, then the entire family, including nine-year-old Ernest, set sail for America. They eventually settled in Virginia, where his father supplied a fleet of ships with grain and livestock.

Ernest too almost went to sea. A visiting captain offered to take him away on a full-rigged clipper. His father consented, then changed his mind. Ernest was broken-hearted when the ship sailed without him, but cheered up a little when she promptly sank without trace in a storm.

He trained as an engineer and became a shipwright but, because of his talent as a draughtsman, he was soon transferred to the drawing office. Preferring to draw sports cartoons rather than plans, he got jobs on the *Philadelphia Record* and then the *Virginia Pilot* as a cartoonist, reporter and photographer.

Like his father, he was a practical man, but also a dreamer. And his dreams were of the sea. One evening whilst walking down a narrow lane in the old port of Norfolk he had a vision:

> Long mysterious shadows filled the space between the ancient buildings looming ghostly and unreal against the glow of the setting sun. Silence reigned. The place seemed utterly deserted and forgotten. Above the crooked roofs and sagging chimneys was a fathomless green sky, and a strange sensation of standing on the bottom of the sea among the ruins of some sunken city came to me . . . I had always been fascinated by the legend of the lost Atlantis. Standing there in the weird half-light of the dying day, I visualised cities once

peopled by humans and now the haunts of
creatures of the sea. What wondrous stories
they held! What astounding pictures they
would present if photographed! Perhaps there
would be wrecked ships, loaded treasure
galleons, rotting in the silence of once busy
streets.

Ernest was giddy with the romantic descriptions of Jules
Verne and Victor Hugo. He had a vision of a drowned world
with giant creatures guarding chests of treasure. And if it didn't
exist, then he would invent it.

In Verne's *Twenty Thousand Leagues Under the Sea*, Captain
Nemo claims that 'nothing is easier than to take a photographic
view of this submarine region.' Later he hands a print to his guest,
Professor Aronnax, who is astonished by the image of 'primitive
rocks, which have never looked upon the light of heaven; that
lowest granite which forms the foundation of the globe; those
deep grottoes . . . I cannot describe the effect of these smooth,
black, polished rocks . . . of strange forms, standing solidly on the
sandy carpet, which sparkled under the jets of our electric light.'

What if he took photographs under the sea? Surely that
would be the most exciting thing ever to appear in the *Virginia
Pilot*. The only problem was that Williamson didn't have a waterproof camera and in those days, so far as he knew, neither did anyone else.

Then with an inspired piece of lateral thinking, he decided
that if he couldn't take his camera into the water, he would have
to extend dry land under the sea.

Fortuitously, his father was just perfecting his latest invention. It was a telescopic metal tube about two feet in diameter

that could be expanded downwards from a barge. On the end of the tube was a metal sphere in which an observer might sit and, through small portholes, direct the positioning of giant grabs dangling down from the surface, to salvage wrecks.

'Herein,' Williamson said, 'lay the solution to my problem. The small observation chamber would have to be enlarged and equipped with a large window of clear glass. There would also have to be banks of powerful electric lights to illuminate the depths beyond the reach of sunlight. I was confident that with these additions and alterations, photographs of the ocean floor and of the denizens of the deep would be possible.'

In 1913 on Chesapeake Bay, with his father at the helm of the barge above, Ernest climbed down the thirty-foot tube into the sphere below and peered for the first time under the sea where:

> streaming banners of clear light pierced to the floor of the bay . . . while in the dim, pale green distance bloomed inscrutable shadows, hinting of mysteries farther on.
>
> All about my chamber, undisturbed by the strange invader of their realm, the fishes swam lazily through the green water or stopped to peer curiously into the glass of my window. Over and over again, I focused my camera and pressed the shutter, filled with tense excitement, nerves a-tingle. Would my experiment be a success?

The photos were good enough to publish in the newspaper, but Williamson was not satisfied with a few stills. Movies were the latest thing, and he wanted to make one. He was invited to exhibit at the First International Motion Picture Exhibition in New York, so he enlarged one of his shots into a print six feet wide and tinted it with a sponge. The public were enthralled and backers became interested.

In 1914 he set sail for the Bahamas with an improved three-ton 'photosphere' fitted with a round window five feet across, and watertight mercury-vapour lamps. The expeditioneers included a professional cinematographer and Ernest's editor, who had abandoned the paper for an adventure. A small crew on the barge above could add sections to the tube so that the sphere dangled at the appropriate depth.

Williamson was no longer exploring a muddy bay, but a tropical reef. 'Could this be real, or was I dreaming? Nothing I had ever imagined had equalled this. It was more than I had ever dared hope for. Down from above through the crystal-clear waters streamed the bright sunlight which, striking the white marl bottom, was reflected in a glittering, rippling plane of light. No artificial illumination was needed. We couldn't fail in this light.'

They dropped coins into the sea to photograph native lads diving for them, but they never saw the divers – they were collecting the change long before it reached the bottom. So they restrained the boys until the coins arrived in front of the photosphere, then shot them 'flashing downward with long swift strokes, white-soled feet kicking, and leaving a trail of silvery bubbles in their wake . . . They searched in the soft white marl for lost coins and looked like blue ghosts in the cloud of white ooze stirred up by their efforts.' It was the first sequence of the first underwater movie ever made, and only eighteen years after the Lumière brothers had given their first public display of *cinéma* in Paris. He even tried filming under water at night, and again the results were fine.

So far, so good, but to secure finance Williamson had promised his backers a blood-curdling fight with a shark as the climax of the film. To attract sharks he needed bait. The natives recommended a lame horse that was condemned to be shot. 'Came the dawn. Came the man and, worst of all, came the horse!' The animal could not be shot without an official permit. 'Suddenly there came the flash of spiked helmets in the sun . . . a guard of Bahamas police . . . The horse was thoroughly examined and found lame. With great formality the officer read the permit aloud to the horse.'

The dead horse was hung beside the photosphere. A native diver had been hired to wrestle the shark. He was protected by a 'secret' oil that he rubbed all over his body to render him distasteful even to the most famished shark . . . maybe.

A night dive of the Williamson submarine tube

Sharks soon circled the bait, snatched a bite and then the horse was hauled away and the sharks 'became obsessed with a maniacal fury and snapped and tore blindly at each other. Good, the madder they became, the better for us, the more savage they would appear in the picture, and the more thrilling would be the final scene.' The diver may have been less concerned with audience ratings as, knife between his teeth, he dived down. He singled out a big shark, swam around it, then dashed in and stabbed it to death. It was an amazing display, exactly what Williamson had wanted. Unfortunately, it had taken place out of sight of the camera.

A second diver had a go, but was not of the same calibre as the first. He was clearly terrified of sharks and shot away every time one approached. Then he hid behind the horse and around the back of the sphere. 'As a shark fighter he was an utter washout,' Williamson admitted, 'but as a comedian he was a riot.'

Williamson ordered him out of the water before the comedy became a tragedy. But who then would fight the shark? Williamson decided *he* would. He had seen the first diver feint and twist like a submerged toreador. It didn't look too difficult. After all, sharks were only fish, you just had to avoid the teeth.

Everyone, including the native divers, was sure he was going to his death. He calmly cut short his trouser legs, rubbed himself with the evil-smelling oil, borrowed a knife and plunged in. Whatever happened, he vowed, at least it would take place in front of the camera.

Under water, he immediately had second thoughts:

> I could count the sharks. Twelve great brutes!
> If only they would total my lucky number –
> thirteen!

I dived, but only for rehearsal. The first native diver had been wise. I would follow his example – take a look about – go through the pantomime.

I didn't rehearse very long. It wasn't so comfortable after all down here with those skulking grey forms on every side. I . . . waited – watching for a shark to appear in the area covered by the lens.

There he was! I flashed into action. Down through the water I plunged . . . With a sweep of the arm, I veered to one side and the next instant was beneath the shark. What a monster he was! But . . . it was too late for retreat, for with a flirt of his tail the shark had turned and was dashing open-mouthed at me.

But even at that tense moment, I caught a glimpse of the window of the chamber. I saw the men feverishly working with the camera . . . whatever happened in the next few seconds, they at least would get the picture of pictures.

My lungs seemed bursting. I had been under water longer than ever before. Now the great grey body was almost upon me. I remembered the native diver's trick. Veering aside, I grasped the monster's fin, felt my hand close upon it. With a twist, I was under the livid white belly . . . With all my remaining strength I struck. A quivering thrill raced up my arm as I felt the blade bury itself to the hilt in the flesh, and the next moment I was swung to the right and left by a lashing body. Then a blur, confusion, chaos . . .

The fight with a shark, 1914

The next he knew he was on deck coughing and spluttering and being congratulated. He was dead beat, but the shark was dead.

The resulting 'documentary', called *The Williamson Submarine Expedition*, was a great success, winning praise from both critics and public. 'The most remarkable photographs that have ever been made,' extolled one viewer. After a première at the Smithsonian Institution in Washington, it was shown world-wide and gave Williamson the funds to shoot more movies.

These were undersea dramas with lurid story lines, sea monsters and pretty women. In *The Submarine Eye* a diver blows open a safe in a wreck and is trapped under water by its door. While Williamson acted as the diver a star-struck shark swooshed by and its wash slammed the safe door on his hands. As this was more or less what was supposed to happen, nobody guessed that he was *really* pinned by the safe. Eventually, as in the script, a native diver came to his rescue.

In *Girl of the Sea* an old murder is revealed by the discovery of a skeleton on the sea floor. The melodrama on screen was matched by the drama behind the camera. Williamson had donned a hard-hat diving suit to play the diver who discovers the skeleton. Under water, as he removed a ring from the bony finger, he was suddenly aware of something far worse than a skeleton's hand.

> Inside my copper helmet I felt something moving! Something was creeping through my hair. I was paralysed with the horror of it. I wanted to tear the helmet from my head, yet, in the midst of my terror at the thing now moving with pin-pointed feet down my

forehead, was the driving thought that I must not – could not – spoil the film, that no matter what, I must go on.

Now the fearsome thing was crawling over my left eye, down my nose, I could see it! My hair seemed to stand on end. I felt cold all over. The thing was a scorpion!

In mental torture, I controlled a desire to dash my head against the inside of the helmet and try to crush the venomous creature. But I knew that at the slightest movement it might bury its poisonous sting in my flesh – even in my eye. Though I might crush it, it still could blind or wound me in its death throes.

No, I must be cool, must control myself. With unspeakable relief I felt the creature crawl back into my hair. . . . And all this time, while my mind was numb with dread . . . I was going through with my part, acting out the scene, while the cameras clicked away and the operators marvelled at the vivid realism of my acting.

He survived to face the other dangers still to come.

The Williamson Tube Corporation had now given birth to the Submarine Film Corporation. Each new film was more ambitious than the last and now he embarked on the project he had envisaged from the start, Jules Verne's *Twenty Thousand Leagues Under the Sea*.

Williamson needed to make Captain Nemo's underwater explorers free-divers, as in the book. In any case, it would be too complicated to have platoons of hard-hat divers striding round until their air lines were inextricably tangled. He sought expert advice from the Chief Gunner at the Brooklyn Navy Yard (as in Britain, navy divers were always gunners in those days). He advised that the Davis submarine escape gear could be secreted within a conventional diving suit and would free the divers from any connection with the surface. Williamson also persuaded the Chief and some of his men to spend their leave as underwater actors. In the event, even they had difficulty with the apparatus, often staying below too long until the chemical that purified the air in the Davis 'lungs' became ineffective. The men became intoxicated, 'dreamily happy', and would 'wander away on excursions of their own, exploring coral caves or picking sea anemones. It was a curious experience to have these hardened veterans go off picking flowers like children.' In one scene a diver was mired in quicksand, but the rescue diver became so 'drunk' that *he* had to be rescued first. Sometimes they became so intoxicated that they 'fell upon each other like maniacs'. In one undersea tussle the exhaust valve on a diver's helmet was knocked shut and he shot up like a balloon and surfaced black in the face and foaming from the mouth. It took five men to hold him down when his brother surfaced yelling, 'I'll fix him. All he wants is a crack on the jaw.' Handling temperamental stars would be nothing compared to this.

The costs were also ballooning. The story required Williamson to hire a frigate, buy a yacht and construct a submarine to play Captain Nemo's *Nautilus*. His New York backers became nervous when, *en route* to the Bahamas, the crew ditched the yacht in Carolina and stole everything that could be removed. A new yacht would have to be found. Meanwhile in Nassau, two of the divers were learning to shoot the frigate's guns. They ignited a muzzle-loader, but it didn't fire – until they peeped down the touch-hole. Their sight was saved by rapidly 'freezing' their eyes with ice and sitting on their chests to hold them down whilst powder grains were tweezered from their eyeballs.

Accidents were becoming everyday occurrences. Williamson, reliving Captain Nemo's adventures, steered the *Nautilus* into the frigate and amputated its rudder. In the harbour one night the galley boy lit the stove with the aid of a can of petrol. He destroyed several of the company's work boats and much of its equipment, including half the diving suits.

One scene required a hot-air balloon to take off from the city square. A huge crowd had gathered to see the sight. A bonfire was lit in a deep trench to supply the hot air. Petrol, having proved its worth as a destroyer of boats, was poured on the flames to speed things up. It certainly did.

'The monster bag stretched with a mighty heave, as though it had taken a deep breath. Then a roar and a flash! Like a titanic rocket, flaming and awesome, the balloon shot into the sky. Hell broke loose. With one unearthly scream, the mob turned and dashed away. The strong trampled over the weak . . . in one mad rush to escape the huge ball of fire.'

Smouldering 'corpses' of shop-dummy passengers plummeted to the ground and the balloon crashed in the park. Miraculously, nobody was hurt, but they never forgot the night when the balloon went up.

There was an even grander fiasco to come. The climax of the film was when the *Nautilus* torpedoed the yacht. A large crowd, including the island's Governor, had gathered to witness what was rumoured to be a spectacular explosion. The dynamite was in place on the yacht and the signal to ignite the fuse was two shots from the director's rifle. He fired a practice shot to ensure the rifle worked . . . and the fuse was lit.

The Governor's party was still laughing and chatting on a boat beside the yacht. Williamson had seconds to decide whether to save his film or to save the Governor. 'Action!' he shouted, and the cameras began to roll.

The Governor's party certainly went with a bang. 'A volcano seemed to burst into eruption. Flames, smoke, shattered planking and timbers were flung high in the air. Debris showered the Governor's vessel.' Again no one was hurt and Williamson got his spectacular finale.

The film was a hit and the scene that everybody raved about was when a giant octopus, its tentacles thirty feet long, fought with a diver. Williamson describes the action with his usual flair for understatement:

> A shudder ran through me . . . I was prepared for it, but the actual sight . . . sent a chill of horror down my spine. The giant cuttle-fish glided with a sinuous motion from its lair. Loathsome, uncanny, monstrous, a very demon of the deep . . . a thing to inspire terror . . .
>
> The native saw it. He turned – struck out for the surface. Too late! Like a striking serpent, one writhing tentacle shot out and threw a coil around the hapless swimmer. Frantically he struggled, but the sinuous arm of the octopus drew him down inexorably . . . How much longer could the native struggle there beneath the sea? Bubbles of air were

escaping through his lips . . .

Into the field of view came the grotesque figure of a helmeted diver, the gallant Captain Nemo. How slowly, how very deliberately he seemed to move . . . Now he was beside the native . . . A flash of his broad-bladed axe – the tentacle fell – the struggling native shot to the surface, gasping for breath . . . A great cloud of ink gushed from the octopus, blackening the sea about the wounded monster, obscuring the courageous Captain Nemo, and through the murk I caught glimpses of the writhing, twisting tentacles, flashes of the axe . . . Suddenly a current swept the inky veil aside. With his body wrapped about with the clinging tentacles, Nemo was battling furiously, while beyond him, unspeakably horrid and menacing, were the great round staring eyes, the huge pinkish body. But one by one the gripping tentacles were relaxing their hold . . . Another cloud of ink enshrouded the scene, and when the water cleared, Nemo was moving towards us, axe in hand . . .

John Barrymore, the movie star, had never been so thrilled in the cinema. The *Philadelphia Ledger* declared: 'The battle between the monstrous cephalopod and the pearl fisher . . . is one of the rarities of the camera. There is no question of fake or deception.' In fact, the octopus was made of rubber with half tennis balls for suckers and a diver concealed inside to steer, to lash out its hollow tentacles by squirting in compressed air, and eject ink to order. Williamson patented it in 1921, should anyone else require a large, latex strangler.

Williamson was impressed by the descriptions of the corals and seals and flocks of fish that Professor Aronnax saw from inside Nemo's *Nautilus*. Perhaps the photosphere could be a window to the marvels of undersea life. He planned a film in which the surface tender would cruise forward with the camera below tracking along the sea floor to reveal the wonders of the deep. When he tried it, the sphere collided with a reef: 'With a sickening, terrifying crash we were dashed against a great dome-shaped mass of coral. The flexible tube bent and, together with everything else, we were tumbled head over heels. Yet in the terror and excitement of that moment my mind fastened upon one vital thing – the big glass window! If that went . . . my experiments under the ocean would be over.' So, of course, would his life. That thought certainly dampened his interest in marine biology.

On his first undersea expedition he had taken visiting marine biologists down and was delighted when they were unable to identify a fish with a flag on its nose. Then in 1924 he joined Roy Miner in the Bahamas to study coral reefs and collect specimens for the Natural History Museum in New York. Miner described some of his exploits: 'Suddenly in the midst of the strange beauty of the submarine jungle Williamson came floating down equipped with diving helmet. Now he advanced like some strange monster with slow, half-gliding strides, grotesquely peering at us through the goggle-eye windows of the helmet. A long crowbar had been lowered to him and . . . he assailed a large branching coral . . . the coral fell at a touch.'

After this orgy of coral-crunching came Williamson's

biggest break. Metro-Goldwyn-Mayer had seen his *Twenty Thousand Leagues* film and, although they already boasted 'more stars than there are in Heaven', they now wanted more starfish than there were in the ocean — an underwater blockbuster. He was on the next train to Hollywood.

It was to be based on Jules Verne's *The Mysterious Island*, his sequel to *Twenty Thousand Leagues Under the Sea*, but the studio insisted the story was too old-fashioned; it should be brought up to date. Forget the cool, cultured, intellectual Captain Nemo; modern man was more complex. Let's make him 'a fiendish madman, a Jekyll and Hyde character, supreme on his impregnable fortress, the mysterious island'. Since he was smitten with gadgets, they would surround him with 'every modern invention known to science: television, death rays, and all the ghastly new devices for dealing out terrifying death. With full control of these forces above and below the sea, he could wreck the world.' For greater authenticity he later became Russian; indeed every character in the film became Russian.

Money was no object. 'Where you have ten divers,' said the producer, 'I want a hundred divers, two hundred if I can get them.' It was going to be a *big* film, more expensive than *Ben Hur*. There would be an oceanful of the best effects that Hollywood could provide: rhinestone treasure, feigned drownings and life-and-death struggles, fake wrecks, phoney sharks and, watch out, here comes the rubber octopus.

The studio had to be persuaded that the whole thing couldn't be shot on the back lot, but eventually Williamson, as second unit director, and a fifty-strong company set off for the Bahamas. With a terrified captain, they sailed through a hurricane to get there and when they arrived there were bodies floating in Nassau harbour.

This being an MGM film there would, of course, be shoals of pretty girls in wet costumes. A minor problem was that the leading lady couldn't swim, so Williamson flew over to Florida and auditioned in a swimming pool for an aquatic double. He discovered Peggy Fortune, a wonderful swimmer who was completely at ease thirty feet below the surface and could hold her breath for two minutes at a stretch. She was perfect, except for the hair. Peggy had flame-red locks, but the leading lady was light auburn, and the film was in colour. She would have to wear a wig. All went well until she swam past the wrecked galleon, her wig flowing out behind her. Beautiful. Then the wig caught on a lantern and drifted off in the current, pursued by divers. It was the only wig they had.

There should have been money for a reserve wig, for by now the budget was soaring into its second million dollars. Quite a bit of it was blown away by another hurricane, the third of the season. For weeks afterwards corpses were once again washed up on the beaches.

Williamson, suitably protected, encounters a mermaid underwater in 1922

There were also storms that had nothing to do with the weather. Directors came and went with the tide. One decided he could also direct the action under water, but pressed the wrong valve on his diving suit, shot to the surface and then shot off home. His replacement had got the first three reels in the can when a brand-new script arrived from Hollywood. There was an animated discussion with Metro and he too resigned. Under water, however, all was going well. In Williamson's judgement, the scenes in the brand-new Technicolor were 'exquisite'.

The film was eventually finished. It was beautiful, it was spectacular, it was a sure-fire hit. Unfortunately, it premièred on Broadway in 1927, in the same week as an Al Jolson film called *The Jazz Singer*. Once Jolson opened his mouth and said, 'You ain't seen nothing yet', nobody wanted to watch a silent movie. 'Instead of a grand super-spectacle,' Williamson admitted, 'our picture was a hushed and silent spectre.' Two years later MGM re-released the film. They kept in most of the original underwater scenes, but re-shot all the studio footage with sound and with Lionel Barrymore as the star. Again it sank without trace. In 1954 Disney remade *Twenty Thousand Leagues Under the Sea* with Kirk Douglas – surely no substitute for a rubber octopus. There were also two more versions of *The Mysterious Island*, made by Columbia, both of them flops.

Williamson was only forty-six years old, but his chance had been and gone. He never again tasted the big time, but he continued to make films and to enjoy the small time.

He drowned his disappointment in blood, buckets of it, to attract sharks for even more sensational underwater scenes. On occasion, hammerheads became so excited they gnawed at the photosphere. Although he tried to bribe the local divers by offering his evening suit (complete with wing collar), nobody could be persuaded to become the bait.

Williamson had always been fascinated by marine animals, and when the sucker fish abandoned the sharks to attach themselves to the sphere's window, he enticed them away with a loaf of bread spiked with dynamite, then blew them to pieces. He didn't learn much about the creatures he saw, and thought that sea anemones and octopuses were related because they both had tentacles. Since life began in the sea, he wondered whether parrots had evolved from parrot fish. The Latin names of the fish remained a mystery to him, but he delighted in their common names: 'Sleek, brilliant slippery dicks, pudding wives and old wives, mingled with sailor's choice; and down a grotto, a wobbly cow-fish came poking her horns through the parade.'

Roy Miner's reef display in the American Museum of Natural History was now the talk of curators' soirées, and other museums had to have one. Williamson was asked to lead an expedition to the Bahamas to collect specimens for the new Hall of the Ocean Floor in the Field Museum of Natural History in Chicago. They sent in an order for 'material for seven habitat groups of Bahamian fishes, with coral and accessories'. Williamson would take underwater movies to record their homes and habits, then collect specimens for the museum's master taxidermist to make death life-like.

They captured hundreds of fish and, with the help of a little dynamite, removed twenty-five tons of coral and despatched it to gather dust in Illinois. There would soon be more of the Andros reef in the United States than in the Bahamas.

Williamson moved permanently to Nassau to be nearer to the remains of the reef. There are tranquil photographs taken inside the photosphere with his pretty wife sketching and that huge round window to the sea behind her.

The commissions became less frequent, but well into his eighties he still pottered in his marine photographic laboratory. Sometimes he just answered the call of the sea and climbed down into the sphere, 'to drift and go nowhere in particular . . . and rest in a world of liquid loveliness . . . cruising along through the hills and valleys, over submarine meadows, through shadowed woods, sometimes in moonlight, only to emerge again in the lovely gardens of the sea. . . . The spiritual influence of the undersea held me, and time passed as nothing. I was strangely content.'

In 1935 he had written a book about his adventures entitled *Twenty Years Under the Sea*. Half a world away in Europe, a boy not yet twenty years old was about to set off on *his* adventures. He went on to make underwater films and, if Williamson ever saw them, they must have taken his breath away.

Williamson's drawing of the rubber octopus

Hass wearing an oxygen re-breather, 1949

(*All photographs by permission of Dr Hans Hass*)

Diving
to adventure

Hans Heinrich Romulus Hass b.1919

On a summer's day in 1937 Guy Gilpatric was spear fishing off
Antibes watched by an eighteen-year-old Austrian on holiday.
The lad was enthralled and within a week had acquired goggles
and a harpoon. Thus equipped, the young Hans Hass first
ventured beneath the waves, and the direction of his life was ir-
revocably decided. He would now become, not a lawyer as his
father intended, but an explorer beneath the sea.

His first adventure occurred that summer when he emerged
from the waves on a secluded beach to the surprise of three young
women sunning themselves in the nude. Perhaps startled by this
goggle-eyed stranger, they didn't run for their clothes but sprang
into the water – to escape his gaze.

On his return to Vienna he constructed a diving helmet like
the one illustrated in William Beebe's books and trudged across
an arm of the Danube under water. The next year he used it to
descend to over 60 feet in the Adriatic. He also improved his
spear fishing technique although he had to square this with the
local police. 'You can fish as much as you like,' said one officer,
'only you must not sell the fish – that is forbidden. But of course
. . . you can sell them to me.'

In 1939 Hass with some student friends organised a diving
trip to the Caribbean. They arrived on the Dutch island of
Curaçao without visas and had to talk their way into the country.
Their aim was to have an adventure. They took a diving helmet,
goggles and home-made fins as well as harpoons and cameras.
One way or another they were going to shoot everything they saw;
groupers, rays and giant moray eels would either be snapped or
stabbed. In eight months they took 4,000 photographs, some of
them in colour.

The diving helmet in use off Yugoslavia, 1938

The dives were not without incident. One day the pump supplying air to the helmet failed, but the diver below refused to come up. When eventually the air ran out, he surfaced too quickly holding his breath and ruptured his lungs. He was lucky to survive.

They met sharks aplenty and found that yelling into the water and swimming directly towards them seemed to discourage attacks. It was just as well.

The police kept a close eye on these wild and bearded men just in case they were German spies. When war broke out they were interned on an impounded German ship in the harbour and were then returned to Europe, not by crossing the Atlantic, but via America, Japan and Russia.

Hass became a student of zoology at the University of Vienna and, although he found zoology 'far more fascinating than the wildest detective story', he was spending more than just his spare time trying to raise money for another expedition. His first book on underwater hunting was published in 1939 and a leading magazine serialised his account of the Caribbean trip. He also sold prints of his underwater photographs and went on lecture tours.

His very first lecture was spiced with the appearance of a muscular friend wearing bathing trunks and the diving helmet and brandishing a harpoon. It was a sensation, but the embarrassed friend refused to appear again so the usher filled the breach – he was a short, rotund fellow scrubbed to a pale pink. His entrance was greeted with uproarious laughter from the audience. Unfortunately, he had removed his glasses and the window of the helmet had steamed up. Blind and waddling out of control on finned feet, he tottered into the depths of the auditorium and almost lanced an hysterical dowager with his harpoon.

During a two-month stint in Berlin, Hass gave two lectures a day and three on Sundays, and boasted he could deliver the lecture whilst simultaneously writing letters to his mother. The talks went well, except when the introduction by a chairman, who had read all Hass' magazine articles, was as long as the lecture. In fact, it virtually *was* the lecture and contained all the best anecdotes as well as the punch lines of all the jokes.

Hass soon raised enough money to visit Yugoslavia, but travel was difficult because of the activities of groups of warring partisans. A local woman gleefully told him that, when they took prisoners, 'Some merely had their eyes put out, others were hung from a tree by their intestines [or] had their heads nailed to the front door.' Even the dangers of facing sharp-toothed sharks paled by comparison.

Until now, on most of his dives Hass had held his breath. What he needed was a breathing device that, unlike the helmet, would allow him to retain the freedom of the skin-diver. His requirements were put to Drager, the diving company in Lübeck that made the equipment used for escaping from U-boats. They provided him with modified oxygen re-breathers in which pure oxygen was supplied from a small cylinder into a bag like a life-vest, from which the diver breathed. Caustic soda in the bag 'scrubbed out' the carbon dioxide from the exhaled air and allowed the diver to use the remaining oxygen. The gear was light and gave substantial time under water, although there were dangers. As the diver descended the gas in the bag was compressed and, unless he let in more oxygen from the bottle, he sank ever quicker. As the diver ascended the bag inflated and he had to vent the excess or rise dangerously fast. Worst of all, as J. B. S. Haldane had shown, breathing pure oxygen is potentially poisonous under pressures in excess of two atmospheres and is therefore only safe in shallow water. In 1942 Hass became the first to use self-contained diving equipment for either research or sport. The aqualung was still just a glimmer in Cousteau's goggles.

There had been accusations that Hass' shark photographs were fakes, which made him determined to get even better ones with divers and sharks in the same shot so there could be no doubt. It was also imperative to organise an expedition before he and his friends were conscripted into the army. His earnings secured a boat, but not for long. It was impounded and later confiscated as war booty. By chance he found out that the university's old research ship was now in Piraeus harbour. So they departed for Greece, a war zone in which 'fish were the smallest things being hunted'. The boat was far from ideal. A new engine was needed and the crew were a belligerent, drunken lot who waved revolvers for emphasis. Eventually the engine was fitted and Hass told a local official that at long last they were ready to sail.

'Oh,' he replied. 'Then you didn't know that your ship is on fire?'

After the fire damage was supposedly made good, they set off. When a ferocious storm arrived out of a clear, blue sky, the ship began to sink. Fortunately they were within reach of a port where they could shelter and have the leak repaired.

The expedition was dogged by misadventure; Hass almost lost his life twice. They joined forces with dynamite fishermen to photograph the sharks that were attracted to the dead fish. Although the camera often jammed or stripped all the sprocket holes from the film, there would be enough good shots to impress the public on their return.

In 1943 he received his doctorate from Friedrich-Wilhelm University in Berlin, although he almost didn't. When he arrived to hear the verdict, he found the university reduced to rubble by allied bombing. Fortunately the Dean's safe had been blown out of the window and was half-buried in the lawn. There on top of a pile of other papers was Hass' thesis. Although primarily about the biology of a subtidal sea mat, it also contained the first account of the use of free-diving for marine biological research.

Doctor Hass acquired a secretary, Lotte Baierl, a seventeen-year-old zoology student whose ambition, although Hans didn't know it yet, was to be a diver. She was training in secret and had borrowed his camera. Her underwater photos were about to be published. They had made the cover of *Wiener Illustrierte* . . .

'Not bad,' said Hass when he saw them. 'If only you were a man.'

The war prevented Hass from diving, but not from planning future expeditions. When it was over, he set off on a lone diving trip to reconnoitre sites in the Red Sea. On arrival at Port Sudan, he was immediately told of a ship's passenger who had fallen overboard and been torn to pieces by sharks under the eyes of his fellow travellers. Throughout his career, wherever he went, he attracted such anecdotes.

The friendly local British Commissioner recommended a site where 'the water was so full of sharks that you could put an oar into the water and it would remain standing upright'. Hass was lowered into the murky sea armed only with a length of picture-framing whittled to take a harpoon point. He also dived on a wreck containing 'enough dynamite on board to blow up a whole town and with enough silver to rebuild most of it again'.

There was one underwater incident after another. He encountered manta rays for the first time. They were called devil fish, for they were alleged to enfold the unwary in their wings and carry them off to the deep. This didn't put Hass off: 'I clicked my shutter, wound on, clicked again . . . the ray was so close that its

wings almost touched me . . . it suddenly took flight. I was seized
by a powerful vortex and whirled aside. The thin black tail tip
glided past me and the sun was extinguished . . . Then the manta
noticed me . . . I rolled myself into a ball and let the thunderstorm
pass over me . . .'

Later, having skewered two large fish, he became entangled
in the line attached to the spear:

> I found myself floating on my back, with two
> powerful fish pulling me in opposite directions
> . . . my exposure meter was pinching my
> breathing tube. If any sharks or barracudas
> had arrived . . .
>
> Together with the wriggling fish I sank
> twenty-five feet . . . completely entangled in
> my various lines and desperately trying to get
> my knife out of its scabbard . . . The change in
> pressure had completely collapsed my
> breathing bag and I was suffocating . . . my
> chest started to twitch convulsively. My mask
> was full of water and I could hardly see
> anything. I thought I could make out a shark
> and desperately thrashed about. I had to press
> the valve several times before I realised that
> my bottle was totally empty . . . I was now too
> heavy . . . and had to fight my way back . . . I
> bumped hard against the rock, but just then
> felt my trapped fin freeing itself from the rope.
> My camera slipped over my back and was
> strangling me. But now only one thing
> mattered – to get to the surface . . . After an

eternity . . . I pushed through the surface,
whipped off my breathing tube and mask,
sagged below the water again after a vigorous
breath that almost made me faint, surfaced
once more and with my last ounce of strength
struggled over to the reef . . . totally
exhausted.

'That was really wonderful,' said the
Commissioner. 'I have never seen anything
like it.'

Even on land he wasn't safe. Torrential storms swept
through the town, houses collapsed and people drowned in the
street or were washed down to the sea to have their heads bitten
off by sharks. Worst of all, according to the Commissioner, the
golf course was flooded.

On his return to Austria, Hass found that the public were
just as fascinated with sharks and devil rays as he was and his
photographs sold well. At a lecture attended by the Minister of
Education he revealed that his field trip had been supported by
donations from classes of local schoolgirls and a masked all-in
wrestler. The embarrassed Minister got the message and offered
to sponsor his next expedition to the Red Sea.

Lotte was keen to go too, but Hass wouldn't hear of it. An
expedition was no place for a woman, who was certain 'to make
things tricky'.

Hass was negotiating a film contract. The distributor didn't
want a documentary but a proper movie with a plot and a bit of
glamour. He eyed Hass' pretty blonde secretary – 'Why don't you
take Fräulein Lotte with you?' And so she became the first woman
to dive in the Red Sea.

She was only included because she was a glamorous 'extra', until on the first day in the Port Sudan, with the temperature at 41°C, they tried out the gear in the hotel pool. Within minutes they had to haul out the inert body of the cameraman. The heat was just too much for him. He was on the next flight home and Lotte stepped into his breathing gear to become a full member of the team. Hass made it clear that she would be treated exactly the same as the men. In her diary she wrote, 'From today I am a man.'

Lotte heavily armed but looking nothing like a man

Although keen to show she could dive as well as any man, young Lotte appreciated that she added glamour to the proceedings. They were roughing it and had minimal supplies, but she had taken along three bottles of red nail varnish. In a photograph taken a few years later the team are all kitted-up ready to dive. Lotte is too – except for her high heels.

They camped in the isolated ruins of Suakim. Until the building of Port Sudan, it had been the chief port of the country. Fifty years before it had bustled with 30,000 people; now it was deserted and silent, except for the scuttle of scorpions. And at night, from somewhere in the darkness came sounds like sobbing and moaning. They never discovered what made them.

It was an oppressively hot and barren land. Cyril Crossland, who had built a marine laboratory there, described it as 'a great and terrible wilderness . . . a naked savage land, every feature typifying thirst and starvation', but he also recalled 'mountains at sunrise, ruddy-clear, the peacock blue of the deep sea with white waves, the light blues, greens, yellows and browns of the submarine gardens'. The desert was bordered by a labyrinth of reefs, swarming with life.

On Lotte's second dive she was left alone by her diving buddy. A shark appeared and patrolled back and forth in front of her, assessing her first with its cold right eye, then with its icy left. She was terrified until it departed. When Hass appeared she tried to tell him of her narrow escape, blabbering through her mouthpiece. 'Yes,' he replied, 'there is something wrong with the camera.'

A few days later Hass planned to drive a school of barracuda towards the vulnerable Lotte. She was to feign slight alarm – not too difficult in the circumstances. Something went wrong with her breathing gear and caustic chemicals were getting into her mouth. She signed to Hass that she was in trouble and headed for the surface. 'Not so much!' he shouted through his mouthpiece. 'You're overdoing it.' Then he hauled her back down to the bottom.

She stuck it as long as she could and then fled upwards, choking and exhausted. 'That was hopelessly overdone!' snarled Hass. But the pictures were fine.

Lotte was besieged daily by sharks and barracuda. 'Do you think there are any giant octopuses?' she enquired nervously.

'I wish there were!' said Hass. 'Unfortunately, the only ones I've ever seen came from American film studios and they're made of rubber.'

They hired a centenarian dhow with abundant cockroaches such as Milne Edwards had enjoyed on his cruise over a century before. It had a hashish-happy crew and a helmsman so refined-looking that they christened him 'Assassin'. Whilst negotiating the hiring fee with the owner, they accidentally served developing fluid instead of lemonade. 'An Austrian national drink,' said Hass, trying to save face. Everybody drained their glass, but nobody asked for a refill.

There were more encounters with photogenic manta rays and with a huge whale shark, its skin covered in white blotches 'like a bed of ox-eye daisies'. Hass harpooned a young shark which was supple enough to whip round and grab his arm in its mouth. It then swam off dragging him with it. By the time it let go Hass was bleeding profusely. 'The thwart and bottom of the boat were red with blood,' Lotte wrote. 'A thick stream of blood flowed across Hass' right hand. The wrist looked as if it had been put through the mincer The flesh was hanging in shreds.' The starter cord for the outboard served as a tourniquet and he was rushed to hospital. Hass was out of the water for three weeks before he lost patience and removed his own stitches.

He had felt the champ of a shark, but the critics' teeth were sharper still. They affirmed that the whale was photographed with a camera lowered into the sea, and the sharks must have been stunned by explosives before being approached. Worse still, the value of pictures taken of animals acting normally in their natural environment was not appreciated by at least one well-known biologist: 'Any good aquarium picture is of greater scientific and instructional value than similar shots taken in nature, even at the risk of one's life.'

Hass had a theory that sharks homed in on the distress cries of fish. To enable him to study this, Philips provided some sound equipment. Recordings of fish noises seemed to attract few listeners under water, but a Strauss waltz caused a school of jacks to swirl around the speaker.

After weeks of showing irritation at Lotte's inadequacies, Hans surprised her on the way home by proposing. They were married in Switzerland and the registrar pressed a copy of *The Road to Marital Happiness* into Lotte's hand. It must have been a good book, for they are still married. But the Swiss photographic laboratory ruined more than just their wedding snaps: they accidentally destroyed several reels of movie film. Fortunately, enough survived to make a film called *Red Sea Adventure* that won the international prize for the best documentary at the Venice Film Festival in 1950.

They honeymooned on the Great Barrier Reef. On their arrival the local doctor assailed them with gory tales of shark attacks – 'Only last week a young couple were eaten in the harbour' – and assessed their life expectancy as unlikely to exceed a fortnight. They stayed in 'a rickety shed which calls itself a hotel'. 'Everyone's drunk here,' Lotte observed, never having been to

Australia before. For a joint wedding present they bought a plastic leg from a hosiery shop to assess the grip of a giant clam, should one accidentally step inside one. The 'leg' cracked like a hazel nut.

The commercial success of *Red Sea Adventure* stimulated Hass to set up his International Institute for Submarine Research in Liechtenstein (for tax reasons rather than its proximity to the sea) and allowed him to purchase the ship he had dreamed of from the beginning. What he actually bought was a 170-foot-long hull. It had been a yacht built in Britain for Singer, the sewing-machine magnate, but had fallen on hard times and was being used for shipping coal. Rebuilding her cost three times more than the purchase price. Hass renamed her *Xarifa* – Arabic for 'The beautiful one' – and that is exactly what she became, one of the most stunning ships afloat, a dazzling white-hulled schooner with masts 100 feet high and acres of billowing sail. Her first master was Johannes Diebitsch who later skippered the tall ship, *Pamir*, and went down with her when she foundered in hurricane Carrie off the Azores in 1957. *Xarifa* carried a crew of thirteen plus eight scientists and technicians on an eight-month cruise to the Caribbean and then on to the Galápagos Islands where they just missed the departure of Hass' original boat that had been forfeited as war booty years before.

Having fallen in love with the idea of having a research ship, Hass did not know how to support it. If you have a ship, there are only two happy days – the day you buy it and the day you sell it. To earn money he became embroiled in an Italian film about Rommel's sunken treasure, but a scheme to take rich tourists on safari cruises to the Red Sea came to nothing. Then a colleague came up with the notion that the ship would make an ideal base for tropical research. The German research councils would surely sponsor places for participating scientists. But they didn't. When she eventually departed for the Red Sea, two thirds of the places were paid for by a contract to shoot twenty-six programmes for the BBC and German television. It would be the last cruise of the *Xarifa*.

The films were a great success and Hans and Lotte became household names. But the yacht needed a new rudder, work benches, batteries, an inflatable, and the decks had to be resealed. The bills were never-ending. Hans offered her free to any scientific institution that would take her. Eventually the *Xarifa* was sold to an Italian magnate and even he had to curtail his other fancies to convert her back into the luxury yacht she had once been.

The essence of Hans Hass was the adventurer, and adventurers take risks. For one trip everyone had to produce a medical

Lotte hanging on to a whale's tail, 1950

certificate to guarantee their fitness, but he took a diver with a congenital heart condition, who was to die of heart failure in less that ten feet of water. For years Hass used oxygen re-breathers because, unlike the bubbling aqualungs, they were silent. But he underestimated the dangers. He acknowledged they are unsafe below 60 feet but they can be risky below thirty. One of his divers, Jimmy Hodges, an experienced ex-frogman, died from venturing too deep. Twice Hass himself passed out under water and both times he was only saved by chance. When diving in the 1,000-feet-deep flooded crater of Santorini, 'An electric light seemed to have been turned off in me. There was a sudden end, without the slightest transition . . . For no particular reason Alfred [his companion] had turned to look back at me . . . and seen me blow out all my air and sink like a stone. Down into the utterly black, bottomless depths of the ocean. If he had turned two seconds later, there would have been no helping me.'

Perhaps he was enthralled by the lure of the deep where death awaits the unwary. He certainly knew its taste: 'Down into the tempting all-embracing vastness . . . Below a depth of 160 feet deep-sea intoxication occurs . . . one loses all misgivings and in-hibitions. The abyss below becomes a pleasant walk. Why not? A little bit further – why not? And then suddenly comes the end, without one even being aware of it. Death catches the diver in a butterfly net whose mesh is so soft that it closes in on him un-noticed.'

Hass was also a wonderful travel writer. In *Diving to Adventure* he sketches a town in Curaçao:

> Anyone who describes Kralendijk as a God-
> forsaken dump need have no fear of being
> sued for libel . . . It is a tumble-down village

comprising a few dozen pale houses, which lie
carelessly and at random along the coast . . .
Scattered along the beach lie the skeletons of a
few half-finished ships, which will
undoubtedly still be unfinished next year . . .
If, God forbid, you want to buy anything in
Kralendijk, you find the astonished
shopkeeper at home in bed. He resignedly
puts on his slippers, unlocks the door without
a word, then, after you have determined that
nothing of what you need is on hand, he goes
straight back to bed. Only chamber pots exist
in Kralendijk at reasonable prices and in the
desired quantity; they were once sold here by
a particularly accomplished salesman, and the
supply is surely adequate for decades, no
matter how brisk the demand.

For ten years Hass gave up diving to study human beings and
their social institutions, which he considered as an extended organism that would eventually supersede man. He thought that filming
us secretly in slow motion or speeded up would provide new
insights into human behaviour. His 1960 television series *Man*
illustrated these ideas, with *Homo sapiens* as a creature seen by aliens
from outer space, much as a diver peers down at marine creatures.
But the public preferred Hass the diver and photographer.

Later he returned to dive in places first seen years before,
including Cap d'Antibes where he had met Guy Gilpatric, and he
suffered the sad nostalgia that is the fate of the pioneer. Although
once he had killed fish to attract sharks, now he mourned the fish
lost to underwater hunters. 'The grottoes were empty – not a

single umbrine [a fish famous for its grunts]. No trace of mullet playing in the shallow water. Nowhere a sheepshead more than four inches long, not one shoal of bogue browsing among the boulders. Nowhere a ray hiding in the sand. Another lunar landscape. A mere two decades had been enough to destroy the once rich stocks of littoral fish.'

He had his photographs to confirm what it had once been like. On his first trip to the Caribbean he had taken a hand-cranked movie camera on a cumbersome wooden tripod, and a still camera encased in a housing custom-made for him overnight by a craftsman in Vienna. By the time he returned in 1953 he had the best equipment then available, including a Rolleiflex in a superb underwater camera case marketed by Franke & Heidecke as the Hans Hass Rolleimarine. It allowed the diver to compose and focus a shot through a screen at the top of the casing. The twin-lens reflex camera also produced negatives almost three times larger than the standard 35mm colour transparencies and therefore gave superb-quality pictures that lost little on enlargement. Some of Hass' underwater photographs have rarely been bettered. He was the first to film mantas and whale sharks under water, and capture the kaleidoscope of snappers around coral reefs and the terrible moment a sperm whale was harpooned by hunters.

Although his expeditions allowed others to do research, the distractions prevented *him* from doing marine biology. But it was the distractions that were his forte. His movies and television films made an entire generation envious of the handsome explorer with the stunning wife and the beautiful ship, and persuaded me that I too must become a marine biologist.

Nowadays, when every schoolboy can recognise a manta ray, it is difficult to imagine the excitement the public felt when they first saw his pictures. Every creature he photographed was strange and huge and almost certainly dangerous – looming whales and smirking sharks. And, most impressive of all, the almost naked divers weaving between the predators seemed so small and vulnerable. Hass never filmed even the most dangerous subjects from within the safety of a cage, for he thought it might induce unnatural behaviour in the sharks. But I suspect that even if it hadn't he would still have shunned protection, for that would have reduced the thrill of his first and enduring love – diving to adventure.

Frightening sharks off Curaçao, 1939

DOWN TO THE PAST

Archaeologists seek objects buried by time. Castles and earth-works may crumble and succumb to soil and bracken yet they remain, for they were firmly planted in the ground by their builders. They leave their mark for ever on the landscape, the scars of ditches, the unnatural symmetry of mounds.

It is not so clear under water. Shipwrecks have no founda-tions; they came to the sea floor by accident. They are the rem-nants of a catastrophe. Ancient wrecks are small wooden boats lost in the vast sea, hidden by turbid waters and layers of silt or sand. Even finding a wreck site is an achievement; to systemat-ically excavate it under water is an enormous task. On land a site can be exposed layer by layer as the soil is dug away, but the sea floor is not so easily peeled. Living creatures or water chemistry may have cemented the ship's cargo into a solid lump. Disturbing the overlying sediment creates dense clouds that blind the excava-tor who, with the flick of a fin, can destroy an artefact without even seeing it.

The pioneers were either archaeologists who taught them-selves to dive, or keen divers who trained themselves to be archae-ologists. At first neither group knew how to excavate beneath the sea nor how to preserve the salt-soaked objects they retrieved, but they would have to learn fast before they destroyed what they discovered.

Frédéric Dumas about to descend to a depth of 210 feet, 1944

The silent
partner

Frédéric Dumas 1913–1991

The story of Dumas is the history of free-diving. He was there at the very beginning. In 1949 Dumas and his collaborators published the first handbook of aqualung diving. Cousteau was third author, a mistake he would never make again. Four years later the most famous book on diving ever penned was based largely on Dumas' diaries, but it soon came to be regarded as Cousteau's *The Silent World.*

Before the war legendary spear fishermen hunted off the Mediterranean coast of France, Gilpatric and Kramarenko at Cap d' Antibes and the Dumas brothers at Sanary. Frédéric Dumas, 'Didi' to his friends, was the best. Under water he had the liquid grace of a seal and the guile of a man. He was a softly spoken predator armed with a catapult and curtain-rod arrows. Fish existed to be stalked and skewered and salted down for supper. But it was the contest, not the cuisine, that mattered. Holding his breath on five dives down to sixty feet, he brought up five fish weighing a total of 260 pounds. He wouldn't hesitate to hunt fish as big as himself. Twenty fathoms down Didi shot an eighty-pound liche, a monster mackerel.

The giant fish, like any wounded beast, fought for its life. It doged and dived, dragging Didi behind hanging on to the harpoon line. If the fish swam deeper, the wily hunter turned his body at right angles to increase the drag and discourage the dive, if it rose towards the surface, he streamlined himself to aid the ascent. When the frantic fish swam in circles, he pirouetted to avoid entanglement. As the fish tired, Didi gradually wound in the line until he got close enough to stab the beast to death. Then he rose to the surface to drink in the air.

Dumas with his catch, 1942 (*By permission of Phillipe Tailliez*)

I once imagined that all great divers would be wonderful specimens who, had they not chosen to plummet to the depths, would have been hurling javelins at the Olympic Games. Not so. Dumas was muscular, but small and scrawny; he looked in need of a good meal.

Although Dumas' family were gentry, his father a professor of physics, all Didi wanted to do was to live on a boat and dive. He made a stab at respectability by reading law at university and was so thrilled by the subject that he never even bothered to check the results board to see if he had passed.

One day in 1939 Philippe Tailliez, a young naval officer, was spear-fishing and noticed he was being watched by a young man, 'thin, sunburnt, eyes of a bird'. It was Didi Dumas. Tailliez introduced him to a dive mask made from plate glass and inner tube, to rubber swimming fins, and to his fellow officer, Jacques Cousteau.

From then on, the officers and the beach bum were inseparable. Every day they went spear fishing together. In the autumn they would light a fire on the beach before they began, so that after the dive they could quell their shivers and grill their catch over the embers. They became, in Tailliez's phrase, the three 'Mousquemers' – the undersea musketeers.

When France was invaded, the sailors returned to active duty and Dumas was converted from musketeer to muleteer in the Alps. Within months France's war was over and he rejoined Tailliez and Cousteau, now in enforced idleness at Toulon.

The musketeers were not content to hold their breath beneath the waves; they wanted to be able to breathe under water.

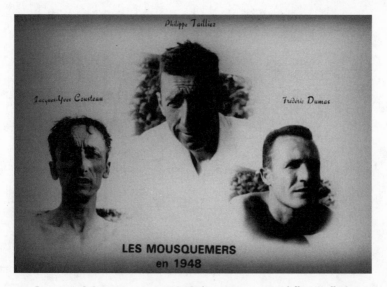

Les trois Mousquemeres, 1948 (*By permission of Phillipe Tailliez*)

They tested a simple device that pumped air under pressure down to the diver, who sucked in what he needed from a mouthpiece. Dumas was using it 75 feet down when Cousteau on the surface saw the hose split. Dumas was stranded at a pressure three times higher than that at the surface. Cousteau just managed to grab the sinking end of the air hose and hauled it up as fast as he could. After what seemed an age, Dumas emerged choking and half-drowned, but alive.

What was needed was a reliable self-contained device that would free the diver from reliance on a surface supply of air. In December 1942 Cousteau outlined the problem to Émile Gagnan, an engineer friend of his father-in-law. Gagnan devised a simple but ingenious valve that supplied compressed air from a cylinder at exactly the same pressure as the surrounding water, but only when the diver sucked on the mouthpiece. Cousteau tested the first aqualung with Dumas floating on the surface ready to dive down to the rescue should anything go wrong.

Cousteau was also making underwater movies. As no ciné film was available, they bought as many rolls of 35mm film for Leicas as they could afford and Cousteau's wife, Simone, spliced them together under the bedclothes. The first shots were of Dumas the spear fisherman, with cameraman Cousteau trying to breathe air from a pitiful compressor on the surface, through a hose that was always too short. Their first film, *Par dix-huit mètres de fond* ('Eighteen Metres Down'), had a successful Paris première in 1942, with the audience full of Nazi officers.

Wearing their brand-new aqualungs, they embarked on a more ambitious project entitled *Épaves* ('Wrecks').

Together with their families they all moved into a villa for the duration of the filming. It suited Didi as his place at Sanary, overlooking the house where Aldous Huxley had written *Brave*

New World, had been demolished by the Germans to clear a line of fire for the shore battery.

First they had to accumulate enough food to sustain them for the six-month schedule. Tailliez was the chief scrounger. One day he was stopped by the police when carrying three large hams, enough to send him to jail, and he coolly asked the gendarmes to hold his parcels whilst he hunted for his papers. He also acquired over time two tons of beans which, with the fish Didi caught, were their staples. As the months passed, more and more black flecks began to appear on their plates and when the bean store was opened, 'a cloud of insects filled the house'. There was wild asparagus to gather and edible snails, and even the flowering bushes in the garden were tasted to determine which were edible. They all lost weight and a woman asked the cadaverous Cousteau, 'Were you shrunk by pressure?'

They dived on sunken ships every day the weather allowed, occasionally attracting a fusillade of shots when they surfaced, from sentries taking them for saboteurs. There were wrecks for all reasons: a shell-riddled battleship, a tug whose crew had still been celebrating the New Year in February, a steamer caught off guard by the Mistral, another whose cargo of cigars caught fire and gave everyone on the Côte d'Azur a free drag.

Dead ships are the eeriest places on earth, existential stage sets with *film noir* lighting, decks and doors at unsettling angles. It is impossible to venture into the black heart of a wreck without a shiver of unease and the feeling that below in the darkness something awaits you.

Épaves is about Dumas rummaging about in the semi-darkness, peering through portholes, gliding past cobwebs of rigging, relaxing in a drowned bathtub, popping down hatches like a frog into an inkwell.

Didi hated to leave things behind on the sea floor. Cousteau claimed that the team soon overcame their early gold-fever, although Dumas had recurring bouts, like malaria. And not just for gold. Dumas, the magpie Mousquemer, wrenched off copper lamps, a ship's wheel, the compass tripod, light bulbs, fishermen's boots and a carboy of eau-de-cologne that he found glistening in the gloom like a jade bubble. He always carried a bag for booty. Beside one ship that was a twisted ruin of iron were neat piles of undamaged crockery and glassware. Dumas collected so much that the others thought he must be gathering presents for a family wedding. Unfortunately, on the way up it clouted against the wreckage, and china that had survived a violent shipwreck and a quarter of a century beneath the waves was smashed to smithereens. His mates kidded him that he might have to cancel the wedding.

It almost ended in tragedy. Dumas was swimming alone along a companionway not knowing that the delicate rubber hose of his aqualung had looped over a loose pipe, like a quoit over a stake. He swam on oblivious until he realised that he couldn't turn his head. Reaching up to feel what the problem was, he cut his hand. The pipe was encrusted with razor-edged clams. Painfully slowly he retreated backwards, unable to turn, his hands behind his head lifting his air hose over the clams. He watched the pipe pass inch by inch and felt his hands become lacerated. Then suddenly he was free. He had travelled back ten feet, the longest undersea journey of his life. In spite of this experience, he now had *two* passions, spear fishing and wrecks.

Dumas was appointed civilian 'expert adviser' to the navy's newly formed Undersea Research Group and from 1947 was in charge of training navy personnel to dive with the aqualung. He also voyaged as chief diver on the research ship.

In 1948 a training cruise to North Africa was organised to

search for the lost port of ancient Carthage. Indulging his passion for explosives, Dumas blew up a rocky platform, but they found nothing. The ship sailed on to Mahdia in Tunisia, the reputed birthplace of Hannibal. Here lay a wreck from about 100 BC that had been crudely excavated in 1907 and provided statues in marble and bronze, beds, urns and candelabra as well as seventy marble columns, probably a prefabricated Greek temple off to be erected beside a rich Roman's villa. The freighter was a paunchy pantechnicon, poorly designed and overloaded. It deserved to founder.

To shift the sand, Cousteau's group used a powerful water jet, but it merely stirred up the mud and sent the operator spiralling off towards the surface. Dumas preferred to dig by hand and used a couple of ancient copper nails he had found. When he had finished they shone like gold. On returning to the surface, he suffered his first dose of the bends. It would not be his last; in those days real divers had the bends for breakfast.

The group 'rescued' a couple of anchors and four columns, one of which Dumas sawed off to make the top for a garden table. Cousteau modestly admitted that they were merely scratching at history's door. No, they were pilfering from history's pantry.

Dumas had found his first amphora in 1939 and gave it to Cousteau for his mantel. It was made of white earth spangled with mica. Later he discovered that it was the only one of its kind known. Amphorae were the earthenware jerry cans of the ancient world, often waterproofed inside with cypress resin. They were two-handled and tapered-bottomed for ease of stacking; elegant containers for transporting wine or olive oil or grain, or anything that would pour into a five-inch neck. Ancient ships were often laden with them stacked three rows deep.

In 1949 an amateur diver had found a mound of amphorae

off an island near to Cannes. Whilst Cousteau was away clearing mines in the Languedoc, the navy's diving ship, *Élie Monnier*, diverted from its mission and anchored over the wreck. They tried out a new device, the *suceuse* (the sucker), now more prosaically called an air-lift. The idea was simple. Air was pumped under water into the base of a sturdy pipe. As the bubbles rose inside they expanded, creating a partial vacuum, and dragged water up the tube. It was a powerful underwater Hoover that could strip the skin from your thigh. The divers christened this bucking serpent the 'Loch Ness Monster'. As gulls follow the plough, so mullet and sardines grubbed for worms in the wake of the *suceuse*.

They brought up amphorae by the dozen. Dumas freed them with a pick. The captain liked giving them as presents and, as he was always making new friends, they returned the next summer to loot a few more. Six feet beneath the mud they uncovered part of the wooden hull. It was like new.

In 1951 a unique opportunity arose by accident. A freelance diver, who made his living by scavenging the sea floor, ventured too deep, stayed too long and contracted the bends. He was brought into the medical facility attached to the Undersea Research Group, and Dumas visited him in hospital. His diving days were over so he confided to Dumas all his secret places for lobsters. One was below the great rock of Grand Congloué. 'You can tell where the lobsters are,' he whispered, 'when you see the old pots.' To Dumas 'old pots' meant amphorae.

Dumas noted down the site for future reference. It might have been forgotten had not some amateur divers found amphorae off an adjacent island the very next year. An archaeologist asked Cousteau to investigate and whilst *en route* Dumas persuaded the Commandant to take a glance at *his* site.

The barren limestone cliffs of Grand Congloué jut from the sea like an iceberg awaiting unwary ships on the approach to Marseilles. On the bottom, 130 feet down, they found a huge tumulus of amphorae, the gravestones of the buried wreck. It was a pristine Roman wine ship laden to the gunnels. On hand was a tame archaeologist (too tame, as it turned out), and Cousteau could muster superb equipment and almost unlimited diving effort from his group; they would log 3,500 dives in the first season alone. It was the great opportunity for underwater archaeology to come of age – and it was squandered.

Perhaps that sounds too harsh a judgement, for it was only thirty years since Sir Mortimer Wheeler had properly systematised excavating on land. But Cousteau considered archaeologists impractical pedants and ensured that they knew who was in charge. For their part the archaeologists were delighted to receive intact specimens of objects known only from fragments. 'Marvellous, marvellous!' they shouted, but retrieved amphorae were allowed to roll back and forth across the heaving deck to clatter against the winches.

The work was not easy. The first gusts of the Mistral were rucking the surface of the water and rocking the boat, and it would get worse. The cold water seeped into the divers' wetsuits. Because of the depth, they worked in 18-minute shifts to avoid decompression problems. A rifle was fired into the water to warn the divers their shift had ended. They had to work fast and speed took precedence over care, so they employed an air-lift. Its fierce suction hoovered up everything in its path. 'It disposed of piles of dishes, grazing on plates and smashing cups to bits.' If the mouth of the air-lift clogged with dishes, it was cleared by bashing them with a hammer. It flung everything into a basket on board the *Calypso*. They had devised a dozen ways in which crockery that had survived the sea for 2,000 years could be pulverised on the short journey to the surface. Even their phlegmatic archaeologist declared, 'It's a disaster.'

The air-lift excavated a deep conical pit into which everything fell. According to Dumas, 'Mud raised by the divers' movements clouded the water, which, being contained within the hole, could not be cleared by the current. In reduced visibility, the excavation got out of hand; divers lost control and grabbed what they could. When, at the bottom of the hole, the air-lift eventually came into contact with hull timbers, the force of the machine shattered the waterlogged wood.'

Yet for all this urgency, the divers had plenty of time to gather 'violets', clams with yellow, purple-veined slime, that they swallowed raw, not as nutrition but for the look of disgust that this performance always produced in their audience. There was also no dearth of underwater pranks. They took delight in teasing the surface-bound archaeologists who had to view their antics on underwater television. The divers slipped shiny loose change into the air-lift, and pretended they were salting away all the best finds in an underwater cave. How much would the archaeologists pay for them? The response was lowered into the deep – a dollar bill in a bottle. Later the underwater camera panned to reveal dozens of dishes each with a price tag attached. A mock auction ensued with divers requesting offers from above. The archaeologists refused to bid so the divers pretended to smash the lot with a hammer. There were several official stunts including a banquet with the crew in Greek robes feasting from 2,000-year-old Italian crockery.

The site was not properly mapped, so they were never sure which way the wreck was lying. It was on a slope and they foolishly began excavating at the lower end so that as they removed the jars more tumbled in from above and confused the stratification. They found an amphora that was still sealed and at a press conference Cousteau and an archaeologist drank the wine instead of having it analysed. They never found another.

Over eight seasons they recovered 200 tons of material, including 8,000 amphorae, many of them complete with a resident octopus. There were 6,000 items of black Campanian ware from Naples, the mass-produced crockery for middle-class provincials trying to keep up standards though far from Rome. There were cups and goblets, dinner plates and fish platters, vases, flasks and urns, scent bottles and rouge pots. The standard monograph on black Campanian ware was based on shards sorted from the tip outside the ancient factory. Now they had entire dinner services fresh from the kiln, their pattern of marguerites as crisp as the day they were painted.

The wreck with its many wrinkles and depressions began to look 'limp and flaccid, like a punctured balloon'. The vultures had descended and picked the ship clean to its ribs. The timbers of the lead-sheathed hull were in excellent condition but rubbery, and when brought to the surface they shrank to a third of their size. The miniaturised struts were used to build a model boat. Some were preserved in embalming fluid under the misapprehension that a dead ship required the same treatment as a dead grandfather.

During the long excavation a diver was lost, as was much of the information that the project should have yielded. Although Dumas observed that 'long Italian specimens [of amphorae] had tumbled down the slopes to mingle with the ones that were shorter and rounder', the archaeologists failed to twig that there were different types at different levels because there were *two* vessels, the wine ship on top, the crockery boat beneath.

Eventually Cousteau moved on to new adventures, with Dumas invariably swimming in harm's way. He was already the first SCUBA diver to return alive from below 300 feet, although he almost died cave-diving by breathing compressed air accidentally spiked with deadly carbon monoxide. Risks were part of the job. One time he sat astride the prow of a submerged submarine and whacked the hull with a hammer, the signal to fire a torpedo so that its exit could be filmed. '*Incroyable*,' said Cousteau, but then, Cousteau always said, '*incroyable*'.

In the early expeditions, wherever they found lots of life they used Dumas' grenades of TNT to bring hordes of fish to the surface, belly up, for the biologists to study. Dumas' incorrigible curiosity led to some half-baked experiments on the effects of explosions on fish, tossing in hand grenades and monitoring the results. One grenade failed to go off so Dumas dived to investigate. As he approached within a few feet, the grenade began to fizz and exploded directly beneath him. He was lucky to survive, only to be sent geological prospecting in the Persian Gulf, hammering off specimens of rock in a swirl of sharks and poisonous sea snakes. The sharks were usually docile, but Dumas knew that they 'have fits of temperament too'. One charged directly at Cousteau, who remarked on the creature's inexperience as he would have found nothing but skin and bone. The divers wore navy-surplus shark-repellent tied to their ankles, but the predators used to sidle up to give it a sniff, so they dispensed with it before the sharks dispensed with them. Dumas tried excavating with a pneumatic drill to speed things up, but it only sped him ten feet up off the bottom. Sadly, because of a broken heel, he had to forgo the pleasure of recovering a large quantity of unstable munitions from beneath a crocodile-infested lake.

Twenty-four-year-old Louis Malle joined the next cruise to

direct his first film, *Le Monde du Silence* ('The Silent World'). As they passed Stromboli it was smoking as fiercely as when Milne Edwards had been there on the very first diving expedition over a hundred years earlier. The film was a superb montage of unforgettable scenes: a kaleidoscope of corals and tropical fish, silhouetted divers descending with pink flares piercing the darkness, dolphins leaping before the *Calypso*'s prow. It won the Palme d'Or at the Cannes Film Festival and the Hollywood Oscar for best documentary. But on the night the film was premièred in Paris, the impassive Dumas, who appeared in almost every scene, stayed at home in Sanary with his wife. Once a venture was completed he tended to lose interest.

Dumas devised the neoprene rubber 'wet' suit that didn't keep the diver dry, but took up water which, when heated by his body, kept him warm. When Cousteau planted an underwater house on the floor of the Red Sea, Dumas supervised from the surface and dived down to visit the 'aquanauts' in the dim depths wearing a silver diving suit and looking like a cool moonlit knight.

The ocean was the divers' playground. Dumas never failed to tweak the tails of sharks and rays or to hitch a ride on a turtle. He harpooned a whale and allowed it to bleed to death to attract sharks. A few years later, however, when the *Calypso* accidentally collided with a baby sperm whale, Dumas despatched it with a bullet before the sharks moved in. Perhaps his change of heart began when he witnessed the great annual massacre of tuna that Milne Edwards' companion Quatrefages had described long before. Dumas photographed the panic of the doomed fish from inside the giant net. In the innermost compartment, the 'chamber of death', the terrified fish charged around him until the gaffs flailed and the water became too opaque for filming.

Whenever he could, Dumas searched for sunken ships. He

once deduced the location of a new wreck from the position of a stuffed olive floating on the surface. But more and more his interest focused on ancient accidents. On the bottom he could spot a wreck where others saw nothing, something too rounded beneath the waving sea grass, something too angular at the edge of a reef. He was able to distinguish a real wreck site, where little was apparent on the sea floor, from a traditional anchoring place where the jetsam of centuries littered the bottom.

He had learned from the débacle at Grand Congloué. 'I realised too late that persistent digging of tunnels and vaguely defined trenches could only lead to confusion.' He now advised archaeologists on how to excavate under water to get the most information in the least time. What was needed was a systematic search pattern with probes, or corers on soft silt, to delimit the area of the hulk and its cargo. Then, once the superficial artefacts had been mapped and removed, the site could be systematically sucked.

He put his ideas to the test on a Roman wreck off Saint Raphaël. Here he encountered two of the major enemies of underwater excavators, silt and looters. Every time they dug, a large black cloud completely obscured the site. Only the first diver of the day saw anything of what he was doing. Dumas had, however, devised a good technique with the air-lift: one diver held the nozzle firm whilst the other excavated nearby and wafted the silt towards the pipe. It was not applied to the surface as a Hoover, but was used like a dust extractor over machinery in a workshop. It was no longer a menace, but an asset.

A trench twenty-four feet long was cut across the site. Although wide at the top, the smallest movement caused its sides to avalanche down so that it inevitably became a narrow-bottomed vee. Beneath piles of broken amphorae lay the hull, with ribs and stringers in good condition, the planking still seamlessly abutting, its tongue-and-grooving held together with dowels. It later became obvious to Dumas that, unlike modern ships, ancient vessels were constructed outside-in, the hull being made first then the frame inserted.

It was 1959 and leisure diving was taking off. Nearby was a campsite where hordes of 'pink, chubby little divers . . . set out in feverish pursuit of nautical souvenirs. They were especially fond of archaeological items.' They waited patiently for the excavators to leave each day, then moved in. When the wreck had been discovered only three years before, it was a huge projecting pile of amphorae welded together in the shape of a ship. Now, 'no longer an enchanting spectacle . . . it was a vast junkyard, a chaotic, dull grey heap of broken amphorae.'

Dumas also returned to the wreck he had explored off Cannes. What had once been a large mound was now a vast sandy basin from which the black ribs of the ship protruded. Deep in the sand he found the slot into which the mast had once fitted. Wedged at the bottom of the hole was a coin put there for luck by the shipwright 2,000 years before.

The looter of wrecks had come to understand that the context was more valuable than the contents. He now realised that the history of commerce and culture lay interred under the sea. Ships were the instruments of the opulence of antiquity. Philippe Diolé put it most eloquently: 'In their ships, no less than their temples, they expressed themselves, in their sails as in their weapons, in their cargoes as in their laws . . . It is diving that has taught us all this.'

Dumas had seen hundreds of underwater sites and kept detailed diaries of all his observations on the state of preservation of the ships and their cargoes. The stimulus to do something with

Dumas with Throckmorton at Cape Gelidonya, 1960
(*From the Throckmorton collection at Texas A&M University by permission of
Professor George Bass*)

all this information came unexpectedly from the librarian at
London University's School of Archaeology, Joan du Plat Taylor.
She was about to take part in excavations of ancient wrecks in
Turkey with an unknown American, Peter Throckmorton. He
later credited her with making 'honest men out of enthusiastic
pirates', but at the time she was not sure that underwater sites

could be dug to the standards expected on land. She asked Dumas to convince her they could. An emissary was sent to parley, her name was Honor Frost.

Frost was one of the pioneering diving archaeologists. Her first dive was alone at night in a deep well in her London garden with only a tiny circle of stars to betray the exit, surely an experience for connoisseurs of claustrophobia. Her first wreck was Dumas' excavation off Cannes. He persuaded her that systematic underwater excavation was possible.

As a result, Dumas was also invited to join Throckmorton's expedition and he set about designing equipment for the dig: balloons for lifting heavy objects under water, a watertight case for a Polaroid camera, and adjustable standing grids of scaffolding that would perch horizontally over a site to facilitate accurate mapping and three-dimensional contouring of the wreck's topography. He also went up to the Lake District to see if a bottom-coring device used by freshwater biologists might be modified for use in the sea. He decided against, which was probably just as well. It was an ingenious machine with ten feet of drainpipe passing through the centre of an oil drum. When he tried it out it plummeted to the lake floor and, sucking air out of the drum, got it to ram the pipe deep into the substratum. Pumping air out freed the pipe, now full of bottom sediment, and brought it back to the surface. The problem was that the device shot up like a missile. Shortly after Dumas' visit it torpedoed and sank the research boat, casting its inventor into a wintry Windermere – from which experience he never recovered.

Spared a similar fate, Dumas was persuaded by Taylor and Frost to write the first manual of techniques for maritime archaeologists. Helped by Frost's remarkable memory, he used his vast experience to make an analysis of underwater archaeological sites in the Mediterranean, and to describe and interpret the organised disorder of ancient wrecks.

Wrecks are not simply the result of the original event – the sinking – they are also a consequence of the conditions they have endured while the boat lay on the bottom. Once the sea swallows a ship, it begins to assimilate it, although some meals have been easier to digest than others. Dumas pondered why some wrecks were well preserved after a thousand years or more, whilst others had rotted away. He realised that the manner in which vessels disintegrated on the sea floor needed to be studied and he outlined the logic of what he called 'wreck formation', how geomorphological processes led to preservation at certain sites.

It became clear that the disruption of an ancient wreck was not a long-drawn-out process. Most of the spilling of the cargo, the distortion of the hull and the decay occurred shortly after the foundering, while the ship was unsupported and uncovered.

'The soul of the past is in deep water,' Philippe Diolé rightly said, for that is where the mud accumulates and wrecks lie preserved in a soft coffin of sediment. Silt is the shroud in which the sea wraps precious objects. It can exclude oxygen so that corrosion and decay are arrested. Dumas had seen many instances of nothing surviving above the sediment, but just below the surface the wooden ribs of the ship would bear every mark of the shipwright's adze, traces of paint still clinging to the hull; even leprous and pitted marble statues possessed buried limbs fresh from the chisel. Anything that protrudes is sacrificed to the sea. Timbers are eaten and rot, the cargo scattered or pulverised by the waves; even metal and marble are slowly reduced to minerals to become constituents of the water and sand.

Without a single formal lesson in prehistory, Dumas became president of the archaeological section of the World

Underwater Federation, and gave future archaeologists a new way of looking at wreck sites and a deeper understanding of what to expect when they excavated. His ideas were just in time for a revolution in underwater archaeology.

Throckmorton typing up a story at Bodrum, around 1960
All pictures by kind permission of Lucy and Paula Throckmorton

The finder of
lost ships

Peter Edgerton Alvord Throckmorton
1928–1990

For several thousand years ancient ships lay sleeping on the floor
of the Mediterranean. From time to time a sponge diver would
recover some amphorae or even a statue that could be sold to a
collector or a museum, with no questions asked. There were of
course expeditions to rescue treasures from the deep, but these
could not be called excavations. As late as 1950 an Italian salvage
company used a large grab to wrench up 110 intact amphorae
from a wreck, leaving over 2,000 shattered on the sea floor.

The most famous 'excavation' was that of the wreck at
Antikythera, off the southern point of the Peloponnese. In 1900
Greek sponge divers found 'a heap of dead naked women, rotting
and syphilitic . . . horses . . . green corpses', but what they brought
to the surface was the arm of a bronze statue. The Athens
museum mounted an expedition to restore the statues to the
nation. They sent the divers back down and museum officials
ensured that nothing was pilfered. Later an accountant was put in
charge of the excavation. Someone more astute might have
questioned the divers about what they had seen on the sea floor

over the years, or would have discovered that their weights were cast from Roman anchors and the air compressor repaired with copper mined 3,500 years before. The wreck was covered in boulders which the divers laboriously rolled out of the way into the adjacent abyss. Only when one had to be lifted clear did they realise that they were parts of giant statues of Hercules. Seventy years later it was realised that a concretion of rusted cogs was in fact a sophisticated navigational computer and its date wheel was set to 86 BC, the year that the Roman general, Sulla, captured Athens and despatched its treasures off to Rome, losing at least one ship in a storm off the Peloponnese.

The problem was not just the divers' inexpert eyes, but also at 180 feet down they had little time on the bottom and their brains were befuddled from nitrogen narcosis and carbon dioxide poisoning. It was as if Tutankhamen's tomb had been excavated 'in five-minute shifts by drunken stevedores, working in semi-darkness, dressed in American football pads with coal scuttles on their heads'.

No one gave a thought to the possibility that beneath the statues and the shards lay the remains of a ship.

With the advent of free-diving more wrecks came to light and most of them were looted for souvenirs, often by archae-ologists. Shortly after the poorly supervised, but well-publicized excavation at Grand Congloué, Philippe Tailliez attempted a sys-tematic survey of an ancient wreck off the Île de Levant, but in spite of all his good work, the tons of material retrieved were never properly studied.

What was needed was a professional archaeologist who was also a professional diver. It is ironic that the catalyst for the birth of underwater archaeology was neither.

Peter Throckmorton was born in New York although his

roots went deep into British history. His ancestors were crusader knights. Sir Nicholas Throckmorton was Queen Elizabeth's ambassador to France. His daughter married Sir Walter Raleigh and his son was executed for sending a coded message to Mary Queen of Scots. It was hardly surprising that Peter would eventually seek his future in the past.

He sprang from a wealthy Catholic branch of the family who were early settlers in Virginia, and was christened Edgerton Alvord. This was a heavy burden to bear and when he was thirty-two he decided to call himself simply Peter.

As a child he was fascinated by shipwrecks. His first school essay ended, 'The ship sank, everybody drowned. Flotsam and jetsam littered the water.' After a hurricane hit Long island in 1938 he collected masses of nautical debris washed ashore. With a friend he salvaged a hulk rotting in the shallows and cut up his bed sheets for sails. They loaded this 'pirate' ship with stones in lieu of silver bars and sank it in the shallows, then dived down to explore the wreck wearing goggles that made everything look double.

As Peter entered his teens, his parents separated and from then on he shuttled between boarding school and summer camps. With the other wealthy kids he went dinghy sailing for the summer, but he preferred to explore the beached hulks of abandoned tall ships. After all, what was the point of tacking up and down Long Island Sound when he could tramp the deck of a 'downeast square-rigger and hear the ghostly echo of Cape Horn gales'? Why 'sail to Block Island in a silly race when the West Indies beckoned?'

Encouraged by the stories of Joseph Conrad, Peter ran away to sea when he was fifteen. His parents advertised for and hired a detective to trace him, but he failed.

Rejected by the American navy because of his feeble eyesight, Peter sailed on Chinese junks and tankers and fetched up in Honolulu working in a junkyard. Among the tons of army-surplus material was a crate of diving equipment. Charley, the drunken ex-navy diver who bought it, taught Peter to dive and, at seventeen, he was bitten by the bug. Soon afterwards he enlisted in the Army Transportation Corps and was posted to Yokohama dockyard. He was not permitted to dive, but was so in love with descending that he even enjoyed unofficial night dives in the dock, wearing a Japanese hard-hat suit a foot too short for him.

An anthropologist took him on to assist in archaeological work on local neolithic remains. Throckmorton used the long navy watches to study so that he could go to college when he was released. Four years later he enrolled under the GI bill to study anthropology at the University of Hawaii. To raise cash he donned an aqualung and performed beneath a glass-bottomed boat for the tourists, wrestling with octopuses and spearing moray eels. He also salvaged propellers from wrecks on the sea floor. Soon there was no time to study, for his business interests now included a large fishing boat, a truck and a huge barge.

One day he dived for salvage on the wreck of a warship in Honolulu harbour. Something happened in the ominous gloom of its interior that convinced him he was not destined to be a staid businessman. 'I had caught something harder to kill than any of the fabled beasts that storytellers put in sunken ships . . . That minesweeper crystallised the interest in shipwrecks which I had always had . . . in ships and voyages.'

At twenty-five Throckmorton enrolled for a higher degree in ethnology at the Museum of Man in Paris. To pay his way he moonlighted as assistant to a documentary film maker and took up freelance photography. 'It was a wild and wonderful existence, and one day I just stopped going to school.'

He became a professional photographer and roamed the world shooting revolutions and royal weddings, fighting bulls and film stars' affairs. He also covered the Korean war and undertook 'some barely revealed exploits in Nigeria'. Not even Sherlock Holmes could have determined which of Peter's stories were true, but this early Throckmorton carried the whiff of skulduggery and to the end of his life he wouldn't sit with his back to the door in a restaurant. Even his family believed 'people were looking for him'.

In 1956 Throckmorton set off to report the Algerian war. French colonists, who believed that Arabs 'do not understand friendship – only force', had overreacted to Muslim nationalism and there was now a full-scale rebellion tying up over half a million French troops. It would eventually cost a million lives.

Peter soon found that they hated Yanks as much as they detested Arabs. A Frenchman slapped him across the face in a bar and, when Peter retaliated, he was set upon by five others. A gendarme refereed by handcuffing Peter and whacking his head with a bottle so that the others could urinate on him. Then he was slung out into the gutter. He was rapidly getting a feel for the country.

When spotted filming an army crackdown, he just managed to dodge the ensuing spray of machine-gun bullets and hide his film before being arrested. His interrogation took the form of pistol-whipping followed by a beating and a stint in jail. It was called 'questioning' in those days. They warned that if he remained in Algeria he would have an 'accident', so he fled to Tangiers. There he met up with an Algerian rebel leader. On a Sunday afternoon outing, they crashed an unofficial road block and exchanged shots with a pursuing car before Peter threw out metal spikes that burst its tyres and sent it cartwheeling off the road. 'Some people who want me out of the way,' his companion explained, returning an unused hand grenade to the glove compartment.

Back in Paris, in a book shop, he met Herb Greer, a young American actor/composer currently acting as a waiter in a local bistro. Peter persuaded him to collaborate on 'a film on bullfighting in Spain', although, Greer admitted, 'I knew damn all about making films and as far as I could tell . . . neither did he.' It was not until they were *en route* that Throckmorton confessed their real mission was to report on the Algerian revolution for NBC. He had been unable to get anyone else to go with him because the French press had painted such a gory portrait of the murderous rebels.

'We're going to report it from the rebel side,' Throckmorton added as an afterthought.

Peter's Algerian friend had offered to arrange travel behind the rebel lines to see the guerrillas in training and in action. To be caught in the company of a rebel was a death sentence, but Peter couldn't pass up a chance like that.

The only condition the rebels imposed was that if any of the pictures were used by the French *against* the nationalist cause, they would be murdered. One night their guide said, 'I would be sorry to kill you . . . But I would kill you quickly.'

They laughed nervously.

'To cut the throat is very quick,' the guide said and proceeded to demonstrate. He grabbed Greer's nose, pulled back his head and drew the blunt side of his knife across his throat. 'No!' another rebel cried, 'You're an amateur', and snatching the knife, yanked back Greer's head and showed a superior line in throat slashmanship. To show how painless it was, he made a rhythmic sucking sound, whilst letting his tongue loll out of his mouth and his eyes roll. The guests felt queasy and retired early.

Another time a rebel demonstrated how good his pistol was by shooting into the ground. The bullet struck the four-inch space between Greer's left foot and a pile of grenades.

Throckmorton and Greer trudged the hills with the rebels and filmed their exploits, not eating until evening in case of stomach wounds. They were the first Western war correspondents to cover the revolution from the inside and to report the routine barbarism of the French troops. It was a major scoop. Their films and photographs were acclaimed, but infuriated the French government, who declared them both undesirable aliens and tried to suppress their film in the United States. The DST (the French equivalent of the CIA) told the British they were communist spies. They would have been banned from Britain had not a reporter from the *Observer* newspaper exposed the story as a lie.

For light relief, Throckmorton spent a month in the dust of India filming big game. As the expedition was driving back to Europe across Afghanistan they were caught in a sand storm and 'crawled into the car and tried to breathe'. They huddled together, while Peter listened to the tales of J. J. Flori who had worked as a cinematographer for Cousteau. Flori's 'scruffy head sprouted out from the folds of his jacket like a badger emerging from its den' and said, 'The sea, Peter, do you remember the sea?'

Throckmorton left them at Istanbul and set off for Bodrum, on the Aegean coast, to do a piece on sponge divers. He heard that a few years earlier a local sponge-gathering boat had dragged up from the depths a bronze bust of Demeter, the goddess of grain. He might try to discover the original location. He never did, but it was the beginning of a quest that would lead to the oldest shipwreck ever found and change his life for ever.

Bodrum was the ancient Greek town of Halicarnassus, birth-place of Dionysius and Herodotus, and was once sacked by Alexander the Great. Nearby was the temple of Jupiter and the site of the seventh wonder of the ancient world, the great tomb of Mausolus that gave its name to mausoleums.

Now, still tethered to the past, it was the centre for the declining sponge-diving industry. The divers knew nothing of Haldane's decompression tables published over fifty years before. How deep to venture and how long to stay down was a matter of trial and, as often as not, error. The local cemetery was dominated by the 'wooden village' of divers' tombs. Throckmorton wrote:

> Before I came to Bodrum and began diving in deep water every day, bends were an abstraction, which I knew about but which did not affect me personally. Then I understood. Understood the saintly, resigned, Byzantium-icon look of old divers, and the savage alcoholism of the younger ones. Understood the thing hanging over all of us, never admitted, never mentioned, but there, every day, after every dive. No one makes jokes to a diver just up from a long dive as he surreptitiously feels his back and tries not to show his reaction to that little pain at the belt line, which may mean approaching paralysis or death, but could just as well be a little sprain from heaving too hard on the anchor chain . . . Every diving job is a race between the inevitable absorption of nitrogen into the body and time, the time that must be spent on

the bottom in order to make money. The
unlucky ones get caught.

Beneath the tamarisks at a waterfront café Throckmorton
met lantern-jawed Captain Kemâl, the master of a diving boat.
Over glasses of aniseed-scented raki he told tales of the fantastic
things he had seen beneath the sea. 'And if it's pots you're look-

Captain Kemâl collecting artefacts from a pile of amphorae
(*P. Throckmorton*)

ing for,' he said, pushing back his cloth cap, 'In Allah's name, I can show you pots.'

And so they set sail in the *Mandalinci* (Tangerine), a 38-foot caïque with half an oil drum for a stove and an ancient diesel engine that had to be scorched determinedly with a blowlamp before it would start. The cabin boy would then put down the still flaming blow lamp amidst the inflammable debris while he tried (often in vain) to turn the engine. The crew sang the 'song of the engine': 'I can't do it Captain, this is the end Captain . . .' There was also an ancient compressor and a single hard-hat suit shared by four divers.

A Roman amphora was lashed to the mast as a water bottle. 'Better made than the modern ones,' the captain boasted, 'and cheaper too . . . We just haul them off the bottom.'

Two hours out from Bodrum Captain Kemâl anchored beside the low, arid hump of Yassi island. Throckmorton slipped over the side and there, only 25 feet below, was a mass of amphorae. The boat moved to deeper water and they located two more heaps of jars of a different shape, characteristic of a different period. 'That first day . . . was a frenzy of photographs and dives and excitement.' They returned day after day and each time found more wrecks.

'The most exciting day of my life came when I shoved my arm into the mud next to a heap of globular amphoras and felt the timbers of a ship that had lain there for 1,500 years.' The reef had disembowelled scores of ships, Greek, Roman, Byzantine, Turkish . . . and they were still there.

By chance, John Carswell, an historian at the American University in Beirut, and Honor Frost were at this very time on a bus heading for Bodrum. Frost was nervous about putting her diving cylinder on the roof in case it bounced off or exploded in the heat of the midday sun. With anti-British feeling running high over the situation in Cyprus, she was also wary of taking a 'bomb' on board, so she wrapped it in a shawl and bonnet and cradled the 'baby' in her arms the whole way.

In Bodrum they met Captain Kemâl who told of an American journalist who had a compressor and was bristling with equipment: 'He is armed to the teeth.' Throckmorton had heard they were archaeological draughtsmen and, noting that Honor Frost was a handsome blonde, he invited them to join the expedition. They complemented him perfectly for they had the skills and patience he lacked. Their presence, and that of the Izmir Frogmen's Club, who were determined to do some real archaeology, converted a treasure hunt into an archaeological expedition. Thanks to the frogmen, the Director of the Izmir museum arranged for their finds to be secured under lock and key in the fifteenth-century fortress at Bodrum.

They used two boats, not just the *Mandalinci*, but also the slug-slow *Simsek* (Lightning). It was the frailest craft ever to go to sea. Her hull could be punctured with a fingernail and the rigging was a cobweb of string and rusty wire.

Every voyage might be their last, and the days were long and hot and hungry, for the sponge divers never ate lunch as it was supposed to bring on the bends. The ship's larder was stocked with hardtack, tomatoes and peppers, and jars containing meat which, if not half-rotten, was entirely rotten. Fortunately they caught an ample supply of fish. At night beneath the stars, they drank raki and told tales from Homer.

Carswell was often seasick and Honor mopped his brow. According to Kemâl, who feared what his wife might say, 'women are bad luck on boats, especially pretty ones.' Later he silenced his wife's protests by claiming Honor was not a woman, but a diver.

Throckmorton spent six months diving in the Aegean. The ancient wrecks came as a revelation to him, and, according to Honor Frost, 'Peter was not one to dismiss revelations.' He was thirty that summer and decided to devote the rest of his life to a profession that did not yet exist, that of underwater archaeologist. 'I was convinced that it was possible to do scientific archaeology under water . . . What historians had missed, the sea remembered.'

Having doubled the number of known ancient wrecks in a single season, he returned to New York that winter armed with underwater photographs and looking for sponsors. But it was difficult for a journalist to impress learned academics and the work was too specialised to be of general interest. 'But,' said an editor, 'if you find something *really* important, like a Spanish galleon, be sure to let me know.'

Peter was intense and persuasive. 'His strong face appeared closer than it really was, and he fixed a long searching stare on me through horn-rimmed glasses . . . He spoke slowly and deliberately', arranging ash trays and cigarette packs to show the disposition of the wrecks. A wealthy businessman invited him to join a diving cruise in the Aegean on his motor yacht. Peter persuaded a Turkish archaeologist and Honor Frost to join them in Bodrum.

The expedition was well equipped until the Turkish customs impounded their underwater cameras, compressor and portable decompression chamber. No argument, however sound, no permit, however vigorously waved, moved the local customs officer. Peter dreamed several times of murdering him. Years later Honor Frost reported that the decompression chamber still sat in a dockside shed.

The Turkish for 'not' is *yok* (as in not available, not possible, not allowed) and, as Rose Macaulay observed, 'yok is a discouraging word that we got very used to in Turkey.' She also mused on the influences that had 'shaped the minds of the Turkish police, in so far as they have been shaped at all, which is not really much'. Unfortunately, Peter never learned the three rules for dealing with obstructive petty officials abroad: patience, more patience – and bribery.

The previous year Captain Kemâl had mentioned in passing that he had found sheets of bronze on a wreck off Cape Gelidonya (Cape of Swallows), but they were too rotted to be worth anything. Peter knew that bronze doesn't corrode readily under water; ingots from eighteenth-century wrecks were still perfectly saleable. So it couldn't have been bronze they found . . . unless it had been under the sea for a very, very long time . . .

Peter found a picture of flattened ingots being offered by a Cretan to an Egyptian Pharaoh in 1500 BC. They were shaped like ox hides, with leg-like handles at each corner, just as Kemâl had described. The crew also remembered 'a spear point . . . and a thing like a sword', which they had sold to a junk man. 'Don't

Throckmorton retrieving an ox-hide ingot at Cape Gelidonya, 1959
(*P. Throckmorton*)

worry,' said Kemâl, reassuringly. 'Next year when we dynamite the stuff for salvage, I'll save you a piece.' The impoverished Throckmorton immediately offered to pay twice the scrap value for anything they recovered.

Peter came back to Cape Gelidonya in 1959. Kemâl guided them to the site, but under water there was nothing but a rocky reef. They searched for two days with no luck and decided to weigh anchor that afternoon. Peter made one last dive before they left, but found nothing. Returning dejectedly to the yacht, he saw someone holding up two hunks of bronze. 'There's a lot more down there like 'em,' he shouted to Peter. 'And a bunch of big flat pieces of metal shaped like ox hides.'

On the bottom were dozens of ingots stuck together. They had passed within twenty feet of the site several times, but missed it, for everything was fused together by a crust of calcareous algae into artefacts *en croûte*, reef Wellington. The wreck had not been so much preserved as fossilised. Underneath an ingot they found bits of wood protected from decay by the toxic copper salts, pottery, bronze axes, picks and spear points and lengths of twisted rope. Sadly, the season was at an end and excavation would have to wait for another year.

When Honor Frost saw the relics they had retrieved from the wreck, she immediately appreciated their importance. The ingots bore what were probably foundry marks in an undeciphered Minoan script and the crosses on a jar might also be Minoan. They had discovered a wreck that was 3,200 years old, more than 800 years older than any previously found. It had voyaged around the time that Agamemnon had quarrelled with Achilles on the beach at Troy, the time when Odysseus set sail for home.

Throckmorton now had something to whet the appetites of

archaeologists. Rodney Young, a professor at the University of Pennsylvania, became enthused and helped him to find funds. He also recommended that one of his best graduate students, George Bass, should lead the expedition. Bass' friends advised against accepting. Everyone knew that archaeology under water was too dangerous, too expensive and just too difficult to yield useful results. What's more, he would have to learn to dive. He had four weeks.

According to Peter, Bass had a 'decent face, very open. He was the kind of man to whom a bank manager would lend money.' Bass had just returned from serving with the army in Korea. He was adept at pool and ping-pong and could dig a mean latrine, but had forgotten much of his undergraduate course in archaeology.

Peter assembled a team of twenty specialists. Almost everyone would dive, under the supervision of Frédéric Dumas. Honor Frost returned as draughtswoman, and Joan du Plat Taylor would conserve the finds. The photographers were Peter, Claude Duthuit, a nephew of Matisse, and another old friend, Herb Greer. Herb, bearded and shaven-headed, arrived on a scooter with folk singer, Rambling Jack Elliott. They had busked their way from London. There was also Kemâl's crew, and a firm commitment from Bass that all the finds would be fully investigated afterwards, a far greater task than just excavating the site.

When they arrived in Istanbul rioters were on the streets, the government fell, tanks rumbled past their hotel and the airports were sealed. Bass' Eighth Army combat jacket was not an asset.

There was never a good time to apply for an excavation permit. Even the most helpful official resembled a toad awaiting flies. But the bureaucracy was so distracted that eventually they got it. After the mistress of a high-ranking bureaucrat 'applied pressure', the permit was a mere formality. It bore only 39 official signatures (each witnessed), 35 sets of initials, 16 tax stamps, 45 frankings and four red wax seals.

The coast around Cape Gelidonya was desolate and arid. The cliffs rose sheer from the sea like a cluster of grey knives. Their camp would have to be at the nearest bay with fresh water; they found a natural oven enclosed in an armchair of cliffs and only an hour's sail away.

Throckmorton had persuaded companies to donate or lend diving equipment and cameras, but he had not secured a single tent. Scrounged orange and white parachutes would have to serve. They were pitched on a beach that was only forty feet wide even if there were no waves.

Bass had got married the day before he left for Turkey. His wife, Anne, joined him a few weeks later. She had studied music and assumed that their honeymoon would be spent within reach of a grand piano, so she brought a suitcase full of sheet music to the beach.

The plan of action devised by Bass and Throckmorton set the standards for every underwater excavation that would follow. Firstly, the contours of the site were marked out with white stones, and Greer made an 'aerial' survey so that a photo-mosaic could be assembled. Then it was gridded, and Bass insisted that nothing left the bottom until it had been drawn and photographed and its position triangulated from fixed points and meticulously plotted on the grid. He irritated Throckmorton by spending hours on the sea floor deciding what should be done next. Throckmorton was keen to get on with the job, Bass was determined to do the job well.

Bass was in a difficult position. He was the youngest member of the team and in charge of the excavation. To make matters worse, Dumas and Frost had made it clear that underwater archaeology should be the preserve of professional divers, not tyros. Dumas had been the first free-diver to return alive from below 300 feet; Bass had plummeted to the bottom of the YMCA pool – once. Tensions were inevitable.

The site was also difficult. The wreck was 90 feet down, which meant that each diver could spend less than an hour a day on the bottom. The boat had fallen into a col of an underwater mountain swept by a rip current through a narrow pass. Divers wore up to 40 pounds of lead or mountaineers' pitons to keep them in place, and draughtsmen had to be lashed to the rock or held down by another diver. Masks and fins were wrenched off and even an underwater camera was lost to the current.

Dumas noticed that a platform over the wreck was hollow beneath. He broke off a corner to reveal copper and bronze embedded in stone. Perhaps, he suggested, a large section of the cargo might be lifted intact. The 'platform' was a mass of flat ingots cemented together with calcareous deposits. It refused to yield to a crowbar, so for three days they chipped away a cavity then inserted a car jack. Even with three tons of thrust, the block was reluctant to budge. Then in a cloud of copper sulphate, it was winched to the surface as the divers turned somersaults of joy all the way up the shotline.

Much of the ship was detached in segments and then the jigsaw reassembled on the beach, aided by photos and drawings. Everything had to be chipped free and then soaked in a freshwater pool, which Dumas had constructed, to prevent shrinkage and remove the corrosive salt. Joan du Plat Taylor, wearing a short white coat like a displaced dentist, attacked the plaque on the artefacts with a vibrating tool.

The identification of several puzzling items came from an

unexpected source. 'That's a pruning hook,' Captain Kemâl asserted confidently. 'And that's a shish [skewer] for kebabs. Raising junk is bad enough,' he complained. 'But junk three thousand years old – ridiculous!'

Many delicate objects had survived: a rope in which someone had tied a bowline over three thousand years before, a basket, and heaps of brushwood that, as described in the *Odyssey*, kept the cargo from chafing the inside of the hull. Then, at last, they found the planks of the hull beneath a layer of ballast stones.

In the captain's quarters aft were Phoenician beads, Egyptian scarabs from the time of Rameses II and a stone seal that was already five hundred years old when the ship had set sail. Sadly, the beads fell to powder when dried. The team were inventing methods of preservation as they went along and not all of them worked.

One day Throckmorton brought up a clay tablet bearing a cuneiform script. 'Wow!' said Bass. 'It's pretty soft,' said Peter with concern, and as he spoke the tablet turned to marzipan between his hands. Bass gasped, then realised that Peter had salted the wreck with a fake tablet for a joke.

Among the genuine articles was a set of scales and 48 weights in three different systems, as befitted an international trader. The divers retrieved over a ton of bronze and Cypriot copper and the residue of tin from which new bronze could be manufactured. There were vast numbers of broken bronze utensils, spears and arrowheads, knife blades and ploughshares, scrap waiting to be melted down and recast, together with the moulds for doing it. There was all the equipment needed by an itinerant smithy, an anvil, a whetstone and the largest collection of preclassical metalworking tools ever found.

The evidence strongly suggested that it was a Syrian freighter sailing with a Phoenician merchant aboard and probably *en route* from Cyprus. Clearly, Phoenician traders had made contact with the Greek empire centuries earlier than had been imagined. The findings would be controversial yet incontrovertible.

As Philippe Diolé said, 'In a hundred years from now, perhaps, men will hold it as a paradox that scholars should have claimed to have found the truths of history at a time when the archaeological evidence lying at the bottom of the sea was still inaccessible. History deprived of the testimony of the sea is incomplete.'

The testimony in the local paper was of more immediate concern. The headline ran: AMERICANS FIND TONS OF GOLD. A few days later a sinister boat was spotted circling around, and its crew did not respond when hailed. The pace of work increased, with the air-lift and metal detector working overtime to clear small objects that had fallen into the sand, before they had to abandon the site to the looters. Greer had improvised a photographic dark-room in a cleft in the rock and could only work after dark. Bass was up half the night examining the latest photographs and Throckmorton kept everyone else awake clattering away on his typewriter.

By now exhaustion was setting in, owing to the punishing diving schedule and the shortage of water. The sun was so fierce that tools became too hot to touch, the sand melted the soles of their shoes, candles wilted and the emulsion peeled from film. And then there were the flies. Everybody got hepatitis and this was considered serious enough to earn them one day off. Throckmorton lost 42 pounds. Bass excelled at diarrhoea. By day they baked, at night they shivered. Rocks from the cliffs fell on their camp, gear broke down, accidents became more frequent, sores refused to heal . . . and tempers frayed.

Sadly, Dumas began to enjoy his role as an 'I told you so',

whenever anything attempted against his advice failed. He claimed that the hardships 'made it more difficult for the members of the expedition to get along with each other, and the multinational complexion of the team only made matters worse'. Divisions between the Europeans and the Americans were aggravated by the fact that Duthuit had served with the French troops in Algeria and many of his unit had been wiped out by the rebels, perhaps even those that Throckmorton and Greer had accompanied on their sorties.

Dumas became irritated by Throckmorton who 'was hopelessly addicted to the chisel . . . although we all more or less followed Peter's bad example'. Even those who admired Throckmorton invariably added, 'He could be very difficult to work with.' Peter confessed that 'sometimes I found myself unreasonably irritable and difficult.' There had always been impatience following Bass' insistence that before raising an object they should check the information just one more time. 'He was capable of holding up the entire job for days,' Throckmorton fumed before conceding, 'He was, of course, absolutely right.' There were blazing public rows, that even Throckmorton agreed were 'stupid and ugly'.

George Bass went on to further famous excavations, some of wrecks discovered by Peter, and became the doyen of nautical archaeologists. Throckmorton now devoted himself full-time to archaeology and acquired unrivalled knowledge of comparative ship construction. He studied hulks of clipper ships in the Falklands and excavated a Byzantine wreck off the Sporades Islands, laden with elegantly decorated crockery. With Arthur C. Clarke in Sri Lanka, he discovered a warship from 1704 that contained heaps of silver coins cemented together in the shape of the sacks that once held them. He dived in the Solent and confirmed that it was indeed the *Mary Rose* that lay there on the bottom. Helped by the Admiralty library, he located almost all the known wrecks of Royal Navy ships in the eastern Mediterranean.

With his wife, Joan, and their children, Lucy and Paula, Throckmorton went to live in the port of Piraeus in Greece and, when he wasn't excavating, he sailed his 48-foot schooner, *Stormie Seas*, on charter cruises to give students a glimpse of the life led by Mediterranean mariners in the days before engines were invented.

In 1961 he discovered a 150-foot boat loading cement in the shipyard at Perama (near Athens) – 'the biggest maritime junk yard in the world'. Although her masts and teak decking were gone, he recognised at once that she had been a square-rigger. She was the barque *Elissa*, built in Aberdeen in 1877, a near sister to the *Otago* that Joseph Conrad had commanded, and the only survivor of the hundreds of sailing ships built by one of the most famous yards in the world. She later became the mother ship to a smugglers' fleet of speedboats, before being abandoned. Throckmorton made several attempts to persuade benefactors to buy her, once rushing to the shipyard in a taxi with $14,000 in a brown paper bag. Finally the Galveston Historical Society stumped up the money, but a further $6 million had to be raised to restore her. Not until 1978 was the *Elissa* towed to her final berth in Texas. A rotting hulk had once again become one of the most beautiful ships afloat.

While in Greece he found a wreck that yielded four coffins made from the granite that gave us the word for a classy coffins *lapis sarcophagus* (flesh-eating stone), so-called because any corpse interred in it was guaranteed to be reduced to bare bones in no time at all.

He was a founding member of the Hellenic Institute of

Marine Archaeology and in 1976 he found a wreck off the Gulf of Hydra that appeared to be over 1,400 years older than the Cape Gelidonya ship. As usual, getting permits to excavate took for ever and in the meantime the whereabouts of the site was leaked to the newspapers and the wreck was looted. Throckmorton never forgave the Greek authorities, and left Greece for ever. There was hardly a country he visited that he didn't leave in anger or was forbidden to return to.

Throckmorton, more than anyone, was responsible for drawing attention to the graveyard of abandoned ships that littered the shores of the Falkland Islands. He rescued a section of the *St Mary*, one of the last of the great 'down-easters' that, under full sail, had beaten their way round Cape Horn to carry corn from California. On her maiden voyage in 1890, she had collided with another ship and run aground. He shipped her home to the State Museum in Maine, close to where she had been built.

His private life was also a wreck; friends became exasperated, his wife and helper, Joan, had died of cancer and his second wife left him. Yet Mark Potok described him as 'the wondrous man who was my stepfather'. This was in spite of the night when 'he pursued me for an hour, trying to pierce my ear with a potato and an eightpenny nail; there was a legend, one of Peter's legends, that if your ear was pierced by a man who'd sailed in string – ships rigged with rope – you'd be safe for ever from drowning.'

Throckmorton felt passionately that it was the archaeologists' duty to publicise their findings, and his last book, *The Sea Remembers*, is the most stunning and vivid account of shipwrecks and their excavation. On the other hand, he admitted, sadly, that 'in twenty years sport divers have done more harm to archaeological sites in the sea than all the forces of nature in three millennia.'

He was also the first to appreciate that talking to professional divers could lead you to wrecks that they had known about for years (as a great place for sponges), but that were unknown to archaeologists. How else could he have located so many ancient wreck sites? Perhaps even as many as he claimed. He was what my kindly grandmother used to call 'a romancer': relatives died or were resurrected to suit a story; a leg shredded by machine-gun fire in a distant war somehow forgot to retain the scars.

He once shocked an audience by stating that the most important piece of equipment for a marine archaeologist was a hangover pill to take the next morning after spending the night in a bar talking to divers. He came to need the pill more and more, even when there were no divers around.

Peter acted as a research associate at several American universities, became curator at large of the United States National Maritime Historical Society and joined the adventure novelist, Clive Cussler, on his searches for lost wrecks. On an expedition off Flamborough Head, they failed to find John Paul Jones' warship, the *Bonhomme Richard*, but discovered the wreck of a Russian spy trawler instead. 'Sadly Peter was drunk much of the time. There were times when he didn't come out on the search boat, and when we returned, he would be passed out on the floor clutching a bottle of Scotch.' Eventually he retired to Maine to raise cattle and run a sailing school. He was plumper now and more mellow than before, but still full of dreams and schemes.

At Bodrum he had revitalised the sponge fishery by getting the divers to abandon their 'hard hats' in favour of the hookah, a mouthpiece and airhose fed by a compressor on the surface. He also persuaded the locals that relics were an important part of their heritage. George Bass described Peter's welcome: 'Bodrum was also Peter's. When we arrived, a hundred hands must have been shoved through the station-wagon window to grasp his; had Bodrum been New York, it would have been a ticker-tape parade.'

But he did not get on with everyone. His life was pitted with conflicts. His stepson admitted that he made 'many friends, many enemies – most who knew him were a little of both.' When a supporter arranged a dinner for wealthy potential sponsors, Peter deliberately failed to turn up and, when chided, exploded angrily, thus losing both a fund-raiser and a friend in the time it would have taken to say sorry.

Often he appeared imperialistic and frequently spoke to officials as if addressing children in the nursery, which rarely ensured their co-operation. Yet, as Honor Frost wrote, 'His vision was seldom at fault and his intentions always personally disinterested and financially generous – time and again, although he was not a rich man, he saved objects for posterity and paid for research from his own pocket.' He impoverished himself setting up a museum for the locals in the castle of the Knights of St John of Malta, at Bodrum, yet years later someone from the American State Department described him to George Bass as 'That fellow Throckmorton . . . who built a private museum for himself for all the stuff he took out of Turkey'. The museum, owned and run entirely by the Turkish authorities, now contains wonderful full-sized replicas of some of the famous local wrecks.

Bedraggled old Bodrum is now a spry, whitewashed, touristy town. Under the prompting of George Bass, Texas A & M University have opened a satellite campus at Bodrum where staff carry out field excavations and run summer schools in archaeology. Peter would have been pleased.

Peter was never a modern man. He was a crusader like the great Throckmortons of earlier centuries. Life for him was an adventure. When his stepson, a novice helmsman, asked how he could possibly skipper the *Stormie Seas* the 1,500 miles from Athens to Alicante, Peter replied, 'Just point her into the setting sun and *go*.'

At the age of 61 he eventually succumbed to the years of hard drinking and smoking and died in his sleep at the old family home in Maine. Friends expressed surprise that he died peacefully in bed – shot in bed by an irate husband perhaps, but peacefully, surely not.

His ashes were scattered on the waters of the Damariscotta River and drifted down to the ocean. 'You must love the sea,' someone had once said to him. 'Why should I love something that has been trying its best to kill me for thirty years?' he replied. Nevertheless, in all senses, he was eventually committed to the deep. He was, in the words of Herb Greer, 'an extraordinary man, with extraordinary talents and faults'. For most of us our talents are merely ordinary, and even our faults are commonplace.

Throckmorton with Captain Kemâl

. . . Coming up for air

The sea is seductive. Even landlubbers of long standing like *Homo sapiens* migrate there each summer and crowd on to the beaches to be as close to the water as possible. What drives us to half-built hotels on the Costa Brava and trying to sleep without turning over on to our braised backs?

Is there in the echo of the surf a reminder that this is where all life began, that this is where we belong? How, otherwise, could something as restless and unpredictable as an ocean eager to drown us seem so soothing?

Whatever those who merely paddle seek, the pioneers who ventured deeper often found something more than they had looked for. As the sea turns sharp fragments of glass into smooth jade jewels, so too it mellowed them. Avid spear fishermen were at first irritated and then saddened by the decline of the big fish. Gradually, hunters became photographers or conservationists and campaigned to protect what they had once killed. Museums that had pillaged reefs to display their embalmed corpses to the public finally realised that this meant that the living reef was no longer there to be explored. Looters of wrecks became archaeologists and conservators of the past.

The adventurers found new, more worthy, adventures. The devil-may-care were taught to care, and their tutor was the newly found, but ancient ocean.

It is not always easy to see the light under water. Your view may be obscured or blurred. But you need not be a visionary; just spit on the inside of your mask to prevent it from misting over, then go down, down, with eyes wide open.

Who knows what you might discover?

References

In every case the edition cited is the one seen, not necessarily the original edition. I have not listed all the scientific papers consulted.

Guy Gilpatric

Anon. (1945) *Who's Who in America*, vol. 23, 1944–5, A. N. Marquis Co., Chicago.

Anon. (1950) 'Pair found shot to death after learning that wife has cancer', *Santa Barbara News-Press*, 7 July 1950, p. I.

Anon (1950) 'Author kills wife and self', *San Francisco Chronicle* 7 July 1950.

Anon (1950) 'No inquest due in Gilpatric case', *Santa Barbara News-Press*, 8 July 1950.

Connolly, C. (1947) *The Rock Pool*, Hamish Hamilton, London.

Dugan, J. (1960) *Man Explores the Sea*, Pelican Books, Harmondsworth.

Gilpatric, G. (1938) *The Compleat Goggler*, Dodd, Mead & Co., Inc., New York.

Gilpatric, G. (1957) *The Complete Goggler*, John Lane, Bodley Head.

Hass, H. (1952) *Diving to Adventure*, Jarrolds, London.

Walton, I. (1853) *The Compleat Angler, or the Contemplative Man's Recreation*, new edition, Ingram Cooke & Co., London.

Henri Milne Edwards

Anon. (1837) 'M. Paulin's smoke-proof dress for firemen', *Mechanic's Magazine*, 26 (705), p. I.

Audouin, M., and H. Milne Edwards. (1832) *Recherches pour Servir à L'Histoire Naturelle du Littoral de la France*, Libraire Crochard, Paris.

Augoyat, M. (1841) 'Note relative au casque plongeur', *Annales Maritimes et Coloniales*, 75: pp. 937–8.

Diolé, P. (1955) *The Seas of Sicily*, Sidgwick & Jackson Ltd, London.

Forest, J. (1996) 'Henri Milne Edwards', *Journal of Crustacean Biology*, 16, pp. 207–13.

Francoeur, M. (1835) 'Rapport fait à la Société d'encouragement pour l'industrie nationale, au nom du comité des arts économiques sur un nouvel appareil imaginé par M. Paulin, lieutenant-colonel, commandant le corps des sapeurs pompiers de Paris, pour éteindre les feux de cave', *Annales Maritimes et Coloniales*, 2ᵉ Série, I, pp. 699–704.

Milne Edwards, H. (1845) 'Recherches zoologiques faites pendant un voyage sur les Côtes de la Sicile I', *Rapport Annuel des Sciences Naturelles, 3ᵉ série, Zoologie*, 3, pp. 129–42.

Quatrefages, A. de (1845) 'Note annexée au rapport de M. Milne Edwards', *Rapports Annuel des Sciences Naturelles, 3ᵉ série, Zoologie*, 3, pp. 142–5.

Quatrefages, A. de (1857) *Rambles of a Naturalist on the Coast of France, Spain and Sicily*, 2 vols, Longmans, Brown, Green, Longmans & Roberts, London.

Roy Miner

Anon. (1953) *Who's Who in America*, vol. 27, 1952–3, A. N. Marquis Co., Chicago.

Miner, R. W. (1924) 'Hunting corals in the Bahamas', *Natural History*, New York, 24, pp. 595–600.

Miner, R. W. (1931) 'Forty tons of coral', *Natural History*, New York, 31, pp. 374–87.

Miner, R. W. (1933) 'Diving in coral gardens', *Natural History*, New York, 33, pp. 461–76.

Miner, R. W. (1934) 'Coral castle-builders of tropic seas', *National Geographic*, 34, pp. 703–29.

Miner, R. W. (1935) 'Transplanting a coral reef', *Natural History*, New York, 35, pp. 273–85.

Miner, R. W. (1936) 'Sea creatures of our Atlantic shores', *National Geographic*, August 1936, pp. 209–31.

Miner, R. W. (1938) 'On the bottom of a South Sea pearl lagoon', *National Geographic*, September 1938, pp. 365–82.

Miner, R. W. (1950) *Field Book of Seashore Life*, Putnam's Sons, New York.

Oliver, J. A. (1963) 'Behind New York's window on nature', *National Geographic*, February 1963, pp. 220–59.

Stunkard, H. W. (1956) 'Roy W. Miner, naturalist and marine biologist', *Science*, 123, p. 879.

William Beebe

Anon. (1953) *Who's Who in America*, vol. 27, 1952–3, A. N. Marquis Co., Chicago.

Anon. (1962) 'William Beebe, Naturalist, Dies', *New York Times*, 6 June 1962.

Barton, O. (1954) *Adventure on Land and Under the Sea*, Longmans, Green & Co., London.

Beebe, W. (1924) *Galápagos World's End*, Putnam's Sons, New York and London.

Beebe, W. (1926) *Pheasants, Their Lives and Homes*, vol. I, Doubleday, Page & Co., New York.

Beebe, W. (1926) *The Arcturus Adventure*, Putnam's Sons, New York and London.

Beebe, W. (1927) *Pheasant Jungles*, Putnam's Sons, New York and London.

Beebe, W. (1928) *Beneath Tropic Seas*, Putnam's Sons, New York and London.

Beebe, W. (1931) 'A round trip to Davy Jones' Locker', *National Geographic*, June 1931.

Beebe, W. (1932) *Nonesuch: Land of Water*, Brewer, Warren & Putnam, New York.

Beebe, W. (1932) 'A wonderer under the sea', *National Geographic*, December 1932, pp. 741–58.

Beebe, W. (1933) 'Preliminary account of deep-sea dives in the bathysphere with especial reference to one of 2,200 feet', *Proceedings of the National Academy of Sciences*, 19, pp. 178–88

Beebe, W. (1935) *Half-Mile Down*, John Lane, The Bodley Head, London.

Beebe, W. (1938) *Zaca Adventure*, John Lane, The Bodley Head, London.

Carson, R. (1951) *The Sea Around Us*, Staples Press Ltd, London.

Crandall, L. S. (1964) 'In memoriam: Charles William Beebe', *The Auk*, 81, pp. 36–41.

Thane, E. (1950) *Reluctant Farmer*, Duell, Sloan & Pearce, New York.

Welker, R. H. (1975) *Natural Man: The Life of William Beebe*, Indiana University Press, Bloomington and London.

Jack Kitching

Kitching, J. A. (1937) 'Studies in sublittoral ecology, II. Recolonization at the upper margin of the sublittoral region with a note on the denudation of the *Laminaria* forest by storms', *Journal of Ecology*, 25, pp. 482–95.

Kitching, J. A. (1941) 'Studies in sublittoral ecology, III. *Laminaria* forest on the west coast of Scotland; a study of zonation in relation to wave action and illumination', *Biological Bulletin*, Woods Hole 80, pp. 324–37

Kitching, J. A., A. W. D. Larkum, T. A. Norton, J. C. Partridge and J. Shand (1990) 'An ecological study of the Whirlpool Cliff, Lough Hyne [Ine]', *Progress in Underwater Science*, 15, 101–32.

Kitching, J. A. (1991) Introduction, in Myers, A., C. Little, W. Costello and J. Partridge (eds), *The Ecology of Lough Hyne*, Royal Irish Academy, pp. 13–16.

Kitching, J. A., T. T. Macan and H. C. Gilson (1934) 'Studies in sublittoral ecology, I. A submarine gully in Wembury Bay, south

Devon', *Journal of the Marine Biological Association of the UK*, 19, pp. 677–706.

Kitching, J. A. and E. Pagé (1945) 'Review of the subcommittee on protective clothing (1942–45)', *Report to Associate Committee on Aviation Medical Research*, 197, pp. 1–143.

Norton, T. A. (1994) 'A history of British diving science', *Underwater Technology*, 20, (2), pp. 3–15

Norton, T. A. (1996) 'Jack A. Kitching the forgotten pioneer', *Historical Diving Times*, 17, pp. 10–11.

Sleigh, M. A. (1997) 'John Alwyne Kitching OBE', *Biographical Memoirs of Fellows of the Royal Society of London*, 43, pp. 267–84.

John Scott Haldane

Benton, J. (1990) *Naomi Mitchison, A Biography*, Pandora Press, London.

Boycott, A. E., and G. C. C. Damant (1908) 'Experiments on the influence of fatness on susceptibility to caisson disease', *Journal of Hygiene*, 8, pp. 445–56.

Boycott, A .E., G. C. C. Damant and J. S. Haldane (1908) 'The prevention of compressed-air sickness', *Journal of Hygiene*, 8, pp. 342–441.

Clarke, R. (1968) *J. B. S. The Life and Work of J. B. S. Haldane*, Hodder & Stoughton, London.

Douglas, C. G. (1936) John Scott Haldane, *Obituary Notices, The Royal Society of London*.

Haldane, J. B. S. (1961) 'The scientific work of J. S. Haldane', *Penguin Science Survey 1961–2*, Penguin Books Ltd, Harmondsworth.

Haldane, J. S. (1907) 'Report of a committee appointed by the Lords Commissioners of the Admiralty to consider and report upon the conditions of deep-water diving', *Parliamentary Paper*, 1549.

Haldane, J. S., and J. G. Priestley (1935) *Respiration*, new edition, Clarendon Press, Oxford.

Haldane, L. K. (1961) *Friends and Kindred*, Faber & Faber, London.

Huxley, A. (1928) *Point Counter Point*, Chatto & Windus Ltd, London.

Huxley, J. (1970) *Memories*, vol. I, George Allen & Unwin, London.

Maurice, F. (1937) *Haldane 1856–1915: The Life of Viscount Haldane of Cloan*, Faber & Faber, London.

Mitchison, N. (1973) *Small Talk: Memories of an Edwardian Childhood*, The Bodley Head, London.

Mitchison, N. (1975) *All Change Here: Girlhood and Marriage*, The Bodley Head, London.

Mitchison, N. (1979) *You May Well Ask: A Memoir 1920–1940*, Gollancz, London.

Norton, T. A. (1994) 'A history of British diving science', *Underwater Technology*, 20 (2), pp. 3–15.

Passmore, R. (1952) 'The debt of physiologists and miners to J. S. Haldane', *The Advancement of Science*, 8, (32), p. 418.

Smith, G. (1969) *Letters of Aldous Huxley*, Chatto & Windus, London.

Throckmorton, P. (1965) *The Lost Ships: An Adventure in Undersea Archaeology*, Jonathan Cape, London.

J. B. S. Haldane

Behnke, A. R. (1968) 'Physiologic investigations in diving and inhalation of gases', in K. R. Dronamraju (ed.), *Haldane and Modern Biology*, Johns Hopkins Press, Baltimore, pp. 267–75.

Benton, J. (1990) *Naomi Mitchison: A Biography*, Pandora Press, London.

Case, E. M., and J. B. S. Haldane (1941) 'Human physiology under high pressure. Effects of nitrogen, carbon dioxide and cold', *Journal of Hygiene*, 41, pp. 225–32.

Clarke, A. C. (1968) 'Haldane and space', in K. R. Dronamraju (ed.), *Haldane and Modern Biology*, Johns Hopkins Press, Baltimore, pp. 243–8.

Clarke, R. (1968) *J. B. S. The Life and Work of J. B. S. Haldane*, Hodder & Stoughton, London.

Dronamraju, K. R. (1985) *Haldane. The Life and Work of J. B. S. Haldane, with Special Reference to India*, Aberdeen University Press, Aberdeen.

Haldane, C. (1950) *Truth Will Out*, Vanguard Press Inc., New York.

Haldane, J. B. S. (1923) *Daedalus, or Science and the Future*, Kegan, Paul, Trench & Trubner, London.

Haldane, J. B. S. (1927) *Possible Worlds*, Chatto & Windus, London.

Haldane, J. B. S. (1932) *The Inequality of Man and Other Essays*, Chatto & Windus, London.

Haldane, J. B. S. (1941) 'Human life and death at increased pressure', *Nature*, London, 148, pp. 458–62.

Haldane, J. B. S. (1941) 'Physiological properties of some common gases at high pressures', *Chemical Products*, 4, pp. 83–8.

Haldane, J. B. S. (1947) 'Life at high pressure', *Penguin Science News*, 4.

Haldane, J. B. S. (1961) 'The scientific work of J. S. Haldane', *Penguin Science Survey 1961–2*, pp. 11–33.

Haldane, J. B. S. (1965) 'A scientist looks into his own grave', *The Observer Weekend Review*, 10 January 1965.

Haldane, J. B. S. (1966) 'An autobiography in brief', *Perspectives in Biology and Medicine*, 9, pp. 476–81.

Haldane, L. K. (1961) *Friends and Kindred*, Faber & Faber, London

Huxley, A. (1923) *Antic Hay*, Chatto & Windus, London.

Huxley, J. (1970) *Memories*, vol. I, George Allen & Unwin, London.

Mitchison, N. (1968) 'Beginnings', in K. R. Dronamraju (ed.), *Haldane and Modern Biology*, Johns Hopkins Press, Baltimore, pp. 299–305.

Mitchison, N. (1973) *Small Talk: Memories of an Edwardian Childhood*, The Bodley Head, London.

Mitchison, N. (1975) *All Change Here: Girlhood and Marriage*, The Bodley Head, London.

Mitchison, N. (1979) *You May Well Ask: A Memoir 1920–1940*, Gollancz, London.

Mitchison, N. (1992) 'The Haldane brain', *Biologist*, 39, p. 135.

Norton, T. A. (1994) 'A history of British diving science', *Underwater Technology*, 20 (2), pp. 3–15.

Pirie, N. W. (1966) 'John Burdon Sanderson Haldane', *Biographical Memoirs of Fellows of the Royal Society*, 12, pp. 219–49.

Sheridan, D. (ed.) (1985) *Among You Taking Notes . . . The Wartime Diaries of Naomi Mitchison*, Gollancz, London.

Smith, G. (ed.) (1969) *Letters of Aldous Huxley*, Chatto & Windus, London.

Warren, C. E. T., and J. Benson, (1958) *The Admiralty Regrets . . .* , The Popular Book Club, London.

White, M. J. D. (1965) 'J. B. S. Haldane', *Genetics*, 52, pp. 1–7.

Wurmser, R. (1968) 'Haldane as I knew him', in K. R. Dronamraju (ed.), *Haldane and Modern Biology*, Johns Hopkins Press, Baltimore, pp. 313–17.

Cameron Wright

Amoroso, E. C. (1979) 'Dr H. Cameron Wright – memorial address given at St. Luke's church, RNH Haslar, on 24 April 1979', *Journal of the Royal Navy Medical Service*, 65, pp. 103–5.

Bebb, A. H. (1955) 'Direct and reflected explosion waves in deep and shallow water', *Royal Naval Personnel Research Committee Report*, March 1955, pp. 1–7.

Bebb, A. H., H .N. V. Temperley and J. S. P. Rawlins (1981) 'Underwater blast: experiments and researches by British investigators', *Admiralty Marine Technology Establishment Report A M T E (E) R81 401*, pp. 1–69.

Bebb, A. H. and H. C. Wright (1952) 'The effect of an underwater explosion on a subject floating on the surface in a submarine escape immersion suit', *Royal Naval Personnel Research Committee Report*, July 1952, pp. 1–3.

Bebb, A. H. and H. C. Wright (1955) 'Underwater explosion blast data from the R. N. Physiological Laboratory, 1950–55', *Royal Naval Personnel Research Committee Report*, April, pp. 1–7.

Brickhill, P. (1951) *The Dam Busters*, Evans Brothers Ltd, London.

Rawlins, J. (1987) 'Problems in predicting safe ranges from underwater explosions', *Explosives Engineer*. Spring 1987, pp. 17–20.

Wright, H. C. (1957) 'Underwater blast injuries', *T.C.E.A.W.* 16, pp. 1–6.

Louis Boutan

Anon. (1934) 'Le professeur Louis Boutan (1859–1934)', *Bulletins des Travaux Publiés par la Station d'Aquaculture et de Pêche de Castiglione*, 1933, pp. 11–34.

Boutan, L. (1892) 'Excursion zoologique à la montagne de Hummoun ul Faroun', *Archives de Zoologie Expérimentale et Générale*, 2ᵉ Série, 2, pp. 1–22.

Boutan, L. (1893) 'Sur la photographie sous-marine', *Comptes Rendus Hebdomadaires de l'Académie des Sciences*, 117, pp. 286–9.

Boutan, L. (1893) 'Mémoire sur la photographie sous-marine', *Archives de Zoologie Experimentale et Générale*, pp. 281–324.

Boutan, L. (1898) 'L'instantané dans la photographie sous-marine', *Comptes Rendus Hebdomadaires de l'Académie des Sciences*, 127, pp. 731–3.

Boutan, L. (1898) 'Production artificielle des perles chez les Haliotis', *Comptes Rendus Hebdomadaires de l'Académie des Sciences*, 127, pp. 828–30.

Boutan, L. (1900) *La Photographie Sous-marine et les Progrès de la Photographie*, Schleicher, Paris, reprinted 1987, Éditions Jean-Michel Place, Paris.

Boutan, L. (1903) 'L'origine réelle des perles fines', *Comptes Rendus Hebdomadaires de l'Académie des Sciences*, 137, pp. 1073–5.

Boutan, L. (1925) *La Perle*, Doin, Paris.

Dugan, J. (1960) *Man Explores the Sea*, Pelican Books, Harmondsworth.

Longley, W. H. and C. Martin (1927) The first autochromes from the ocean bottom. National Geographic January 1927, pp. 56–60.

Pohl, L. (1934) 'Louis Boutan', *Bulletin de la Société d'Océanographie de France*, 14ᵉ anneé, 78, pp. 1372–5.

Pohl, L. (1936) 'Hommage à Louis Boutan', *Notes de l'Institut Océanographique de L'Indochine*, 31, pp. 7–14.

Thompson, W. (1856) 'On taking photographic images under water', *Journal of the Society of Arts*, 9 May 1856.

Vincent, J. (1998) 'Biomimetics: technology imitating nature', *Biologist*, 45, pp. 57–61.

John Williamson

Aubry, Y. (1996) 'Williamson magicien de la mer', in J. E. Williamson, *Vingt Ans Sous les Mers*, Éditions Jean-Michel Place, Paris.

Dugan, J. (1960) *Man Explores the Sea*, Pelican Books, Harmondsworth.

Miner, R. W. (1924) 'Hunting corals in the Bahamas', *Natural History*, New York, 24, pp. 595–600.

Verne, J. (1875) *Twenty Thousand Leagues Under the Sea; or The Marvellous and Exciting Adventure of Pierre Aronnax, Conseil his Servant, and Ned Land, a Canadian Harpooner*, G. M. Smith, Boston.

Williamson, J. E. (1935) *Twenty Years Under the Sea*, John Lane, The Bodley Head, London.

Hans Hass

Crossland, C. (1913) *Desert and Water Gardens of the Red Sea*, Cambridge University Press.

Hass, H. (1948) 'Beiträge zur Kenntnis der Reteporiden mit besonderer Berücksichtigung der Formbildungsgesetze ihrer Zoarien und einen Bericht über die darbei angewandte neue Methode für Untersuchungen auf dem Meeresgrund', *Zoologica*, Stuttgart, 57, pp. 1–138.

Hass, H. (1952) *Diving to Adventure*, Jarrolds, London.

Hass, H. (1952) *Under the Red Sea*, Jarrolds, London.

Hass, H. (1954) *Men and Sharks*, Jarrolds, London.

Hass, H. (1958) *We Come from the Sea*, Jarrolds, London.

Hass, H. (1970) *The Human Animal. The Mystery of Man's Behaviour*, Hodder & Stoughton Ltd, London.

Hass, H. (1972) *To Unplumbed Depths*, Harrap & Co. Ltd, London.

Hass, L. (1972) *Girl on the Ocean Floor*, Harrap & Co. Ltd, London.

Frédéric Dumas

Cousteau, J. Y., with F. Dumas (1953) *The Silent World*, Hamish Hamilton, London.

Cousteau, J. Y. (1954) 'Fish men discover a 2,200-year-old Greek ship', *National Geographic*, January 1954, pp. 1–36.

Cousteau, J. Y., with J. Dugan (1963) *The Living Sea*, Hamish Hamilton, London.

Diolé, P. (1954) *4,000 Years Under the Sea*, Sidgwick & Jackson, London.

Diolé, P., and A. Falco (1976) *The Memoirs of Falco, Chief Diver of the Calypso*, Cassell, London.

Dugan, J. (1960) *Man Explores the Sea*, Pelican Books, Harmondsworth.

Dumas, F. (1965) 'Underwater work and archaeological problems', in J. du P. Taylor (ed.), *Marine Archaeology*, Hutchinson, London, pp. 15–23.

Dumas, F. (1976) *30 Centuries Under the Sea*, Crown Publishers, New York.

Frost, H. (1963) *Under the Mediterranean*, Routledge, London.

Frost, H. (1992) 'In memory of Frédéric Dumas', *International Journal of Nautical Archaeology*, 21, pp. 1–3.

Smith, G. (ed.) (1969) *Letters of Aldous Huxley*, Chatto & Windus, London.

Tailliez, P. (1954) *To Hidden Depths*, William Kimber, London.

Tazieff, H. (1956) *South from the Red Sea*, Lutterworth Press, London.

Throckmorton, P. (1965) *The Lost Ships, An Adventure in Undersea Archaeology*, Jonathan Cape, London.

Throckmorton, P. (1996) *The Sea Remembers. Shipwrecks and Archaeology*, Chancellor Press, London.

Peter Throckmorton

Anon. (1990) 'Peter Throckmorton', *Daily Telegraph*, 2 July 1990.

Bass, G. F. (1965) 'Cape Gelidonya: preliminary report', in J. du P. Taylor (ed.), *Marine Archaeology*, Hutchinson, London, pp. 119–40.

Bass, G. F. (1975) *Archaeology Beneath the Sea*, Walker & Co., New York.

Bass, G. F., and P. Throckmorton (1961) 'Excavating a Bronze Age shipwreck', *Archaeology*, 14, (2), pp. 78–87.

Bound, M. (1991) 'The rescue of the Down Easter 'St Mary' in the Falkland Islands', *Enalia*, supplement 2, pp. 5–14.

Diolé, P. (1954) *4,000 Years Under the Sea*, Sidgwick & Jackson Ltd, London.

Dumas, F. (1976) *30 Centuries Under the Sea*, Crown Publishers, New York.

Frost, H. (1963) *Under the Mediterranean*, Routledge, London.

Frost, H. (1990) 'Personal memories of Peter Throckmorton', *International Journal of Nautical Archaeology*, 19, pp. 181–2.

Greer, H. (1962) *A Scattering of Dust*, Hutchinson, London.

Kritzas, H. (1991) 'Peter Throckmorton, an Odysseus of the deep', *Enalia*, supplement 2, pp. 15–23.

Macaulay, R. (1956) *The Towers of Trebizond*, William Collins Sons & Co. Ltd, London.

Marsden, P. (1990) 'Peter Throckmorton', *The Independent*, 21 June 1990.

Phelps, W. (1990) 'Peter Throckmorton', *Enalia Annual I*.

Potok, M. (1993) *Sea of Love*, D. Magazine, pp. 28–9.

Throckmorton, P. (1960) 'Thirty-three centuries under the sea', *National Geographic*, May 1960, pp. 682–703.

Throckmorton, P. (1962) 'Oldest known shipwreck yields Bronze Age cargo', *National Geographic*, May 1962, pp. 697–711.

Throckmorton, P. (1965) *The Lost Ships. An Adventure in Undersea Archaeology*, Jonathan Cape, London.

Throckmorton, P. (1977) *Diving for Treasure*, Thames & Hudson, London.

Throckmorton, P. (1996) *The Sea Remembers. Shipwrecks and Archaeology*, Chancellor Press, London.

Credits

The author would like to thank all those responsible for giving permission to reproduce extracts from the following copyright material:

Otis Barton (1954) *Adventure on Land and Under the Sea*. Century Press. Reprinted by permission of Gillon Aitkin Associates Ltd., London.

George Bass (1975) *Archaeology Beneath the Sea*. Reprinted by permission of Walker & Co., New York.

William Beebe (1935) *Half Mile Down*. John Lane The Bodley Head, London. Reprinted by permission of Random House UK Ltd.

William Beebe (1938) *Zaca Adventure*. John Lane The Bodley Head, London. Reprinted by permission of Random House UK Ltd.

Paul Brickhill (1951) *The Dam Busters*. Evans Bros, London. Reprinted by permission of David Higman Associates.

Ronald Clarke (1968) *J. B. S. The life and work of J. B. S. Haldane*. Hodder & Stoughton, London. Reprinted by permission of Peters Fraser & Dunlop Group Ltd on behalf of © 1968 Ronald Clark.

Cyril Crossland (1913) *Desert and Water Gardens of the Red Sea*. Reprinted by permission of Cambridge University Press.

Jacques Y. Cousteau (1954) Fish men discover a 2200-year-old Greek ship. *National Geographic*. Reprinted by permission of the National Geographic Society, Washington, D.C.

Frédéric Dumas (1976) *30 Centuries Under the Sea*. Reprinted by permission of The Crown Publishing Group, New York. © 1976 Frédéric Dumas.

Honor Frost (1963) *Under the Mediterranean*. Routledge & Kegan Paul. Reprinted by permission of Routledge. © 1963 Honor Frost.

Herb Greer (1962) *A Scattering of Dust*. Hutchinson, London. Reprinted by kind permission of Herb Greer.

J. B. S. Haldane (1923) *Daedalus or Science and the Future*, p.III, Kegan, Paul, Trench & Trubner, London. Reprinted by permission of Routledge.

J. B. S. Haldane (1941) *Human Life and Death at High Pressure*. Reprinted by permission from Nature, © 1941, Macmillan Magazines Ltd, and Professor J. Murdock Mitchison.

L. K. Haldane (1961) *Friends and Kindred*. Faber & Faber, London. Reprinted by kind permission of Professor J. Murdock Mitchison.

Hans Hass (1952) *Diving to Adventure*. Jarrolds, London. Reprinted by kind permission of Hans & Lotte Hass.

Hans Hass (1952) *Under the Red Sea*. Jarrolds, London. Reprinted by kind permission of Hans & Lotte Hass.

Hans Hass (1954) *Men and Sharks*. Jarrolds, London. Reprinted by kind permission of Hans & Lotte Hass.

Hans Hass (1972) *To Unplumbed Depths*. Harrap & Co. Ltd, London. Reprinted by kind permission of Hans & Lotte Hass.

Lotte Hass (1972) *Girl on the Ocean Floor*. Harrap & Co. Ltd, London. Reprinted by kind permission of Hans & Lotte Hass.

Aldous Huxley (1928) *Point Counter Point*. Chatto & Windus Ltd., London. Reprinted by permission of Random House UK Ltd.

Aldous Huxley (1923) *Antic Hay*. Chatto & Windus, London. Reprinted by permission of Random House UK Ltd.

J. A. Kitching (1941) Studies in sublittoral ecology III. Laminaria forest on the west coast of Scotland; a study of zonation in relation to wave action and illumination. Reprinted by permission of the Biological Bulletin, Woods Hole.

Rose Macauley (1956) *The Towers of Trebizond*. William Collins Sons & Co. Ltd., London. Reprinted by permission of HarperCollins Publishers, London.

Roy W. Miner (1936) Sea creatures of our Atlantic shores. *National Geographic*. Reprinted by permission of the National Geographic Society, Washington, D.C.

Roy W. Miner (1938) On the bottom of a south sea pearl lagoon. *National Geographic*. Reprinted by permission of the National Geographic Society, Washington, D.C.

Naomi Mitchison (1973) *Small Talk: Memories of an Edwardian Childhood*. The Bodley Head, London. Reprinted by permission of David Higman Associates.

Naomi Mitchison (1975) *All Change Here: Girlhood and Marriage*. The Bodley Head, London. Reprinted by permission of David Higman Associates.

Naomi Mitchison (1979) *You May Well Ask: A Memoir 1920-1940*. Gollancz, London. Reprinted by permission of David Higham Associates.

G. Smith, Editor (1969) *Letters of Aldous Huxley*. Chatto & Windus, London. Reprinted by permission of Random House UK Ltd.

Mark Potok (1993) *Sea of Love*. Reprinted by permission of D Magazine, Dallas.

Dorothy Sheridan, Editor (1985) *Among You Taking Notes . . . The wartime diaries of Naomi Mitchison*. Gollancz, London. Reprinted with permission of Curtis Brown Ltd., London. Copyright of the Trustees of the Mass-Observation Archive at the University of Sussex.

Peter Throckmorton (1960) Thirty three centuries under the sea. *National Geographic*. Reprinted by permission of the National Geographic Society, Washington, D.C.

Peter Throckmorton (1962) Oldest known shipwreck yields bronze age cargo. *National Geographic*. Reprinted by permission of the National Geographic Society, Washington, D.C.

Peter Throckmorton (1965) *The Lost Ships. An Adventure in Undersea*

Archaeology. Jonathan Cape, London. Reprinted by kind permission of Lucy & Paula Throckmorton.

Peter Throckmorton (1977) *Diving for Treasure.* Thames & Hudson, London. Reprinted by permission of Thames & Hudson. © 1977 Peter Throckmorton.

J. Ernest Williamson (1935) *Twenty Years Under the Sea.* John Lane, The Bodley Head, London. Reprinted by kind permission of Sylvia Munro.